EV CHARGING DONE RIGHT

The Promises and Perils of Offering Electric Vehicle Charging Services

John P. Mitton

AUTHOR'S NOTE

This book is sold with the understanding that neither the author nor the publisher is engaged in rendering legal, engineering, investment, or accounting services. The information, ideas, and suggestions contained herein have been developed from sources, including publications and research, that are considered and believed to be reliable but cannot be guaranteed insofar as they apply to any particular property owner or investor. Moreover, because of the technical nature of the material and the fact that the electric vehicle industry is ever changing, the assistance of a qualified attorney, engineer, investment advisor, or accountant is recommended when implementing any plans or ideas discussed in this book. The author specifically disclaims any liability, loss, or risk, personal or otherwise, incurred as a consequence, directly or indirectly, of the use and application of any of the techniques or contents of this book.

Copyright © 2024 by John P. Mitton.

All rights reserved. No part of this book may be reproduced or transmitted in any form by any means (electronic, photocopying, recording, or otherwise) without the prior written permission of the author. This book and the individual images contained within are protected under the laws of the United States and other countries. Unauthorized use may result in civil liability and criminal prosecution.

Copy editor and typesetter: Emily V. Rogers
Cover designer: Sheri Mueller

CONTENTS

Introduction . . . . **vii**
    Charging Profitability Matrix viii
    Book Notes. xii

1. Outsource vs. Own & Operate **1**
    Outsourced Business Model 3
    Own & Operate Model 5

2. Finding the Money **11**
    Tax Credits 13
    Utility Reimbursements 16
    Government Grants 18
    Clean Fuel Standard Credits 19

3. Site Selection **23**
    High Voltage Power Availability 24
    Potential Charging Volume 28
    Reasonable Utility Rates 31
    Other Feasibility Considerations 32

4. Getting a Grip on Utility Rates **33**
    Energy Fees and Demand Fees 35
    A Tale of Two Charging Facilities 37
    Special EV Charging Rates 40
    Time-of-Use Rates 42
    You Might Have Two Utilities 43
    Utility-Owned Chargers 43
    On-Site Power Generation 44
    Energy Service Companies (ESCOs) 45

5. Equipment Selection **47**
    Legal Requirements. 49
    "Must-Have" Features 51
    "Nice-to-Have" Features 58
    Battery Buffering. 59
    Equipment Reviews 62
    Future-Proofing 63

6. Charging Network Selection **67**
    OCPP: Open Charge Point Protocol 68
    CPO Business Models 69
    Vetting and Selection 71
    Legal and Incentive Considerations 72

7. Federal NEVI & CFI Funding 75
- Applying for NEVI Grants 77
- Applying for CFI Grants 80

8. Modeling Return on Investment 83
- Modeling Tools 84
- Elements of the Model 85
- Building an ROI Model 89

9. Why So Many Chargers Are Broken . . 101
- Oversight and Accountability 102
- What Is Being Done about It 105
- Reliability Tips for Your Charging Facility . .106

10. Level 2 Charging Considerations . . . 113
- ROI Modeling 113
- Utility Cost Mitigation 114
- Dynamic Load and Branch Circuit Balancing . .114
- Networking 115

11. The Road Ahead 117

Index of Terms & Abbreviations 119

INTRODUCTION

So you are thinking about offering EV charging at your business or workplace? Well, spend an hour or two with this book and I will help you get your bearings. For the past few years, I have worked closely with property owners, equipment suppliers, network providers, engineering firms, electrical contractors, and investors as they have set up charging facilities around the country. Prior to this, I spent two decades developing and investing in other alternative fuel projects (especially natural gas vehicles) that exhibited similar risks and rewards. And as far as I know, this is the first book to clear the fog surrounding what to expect as a public charging facility owner when it comes to the risks and potential returns.

Allow me to first state that I'm neither an EV advocate nor opponent. There are many voices out there debating the merits of electric vehicles generally, and it isn't my intent to wade into those muddy waters. My assumption is that you picked up this book because offering charging to your customers or employees seems like something worth looking into; or maybe because it is becoming required of your business—such as auto dealerships are now finding. Rather than convince you one way or the other, my intent is to provide an *unbiased* resource to assist in deciding if this is the right move, and how to go about doing it profitably should you embark on the journey.

The focus of the book is on DC fast-charging facilities serving the general public, although those who manage fleet vehicles and those offering slower Level 2 AC chargers will also benefit from information provided as to site selection, financial incentives, codes, standards, and utility rate structures. I provide some specific advice on Level 2 charging in chapter 10.

CHARGING PROFITABILITY MATRIX

If you learn nothing else from this book, know that there are four elements in play in determining if a new fast-charging facility might be worth the investment. I refer to this as the *Charging Profitability Matrix* throughout the book:

Potential Charging Volume (Chapter 3)	**Utility Demand Fees** (Chapters 4 & 5)
MIN. CRITERIA: 8+ sessions / charger / day	MIN. CRITERIA: $10/kW or lower
IF NOT: Consider building a smaller facility	IF NOT: Consider on-site battery buffering
Grants, Incentives, Tax Credits (Chapter 2)	**Energy Cost & Availability** (Chapters 3 & 4)
MIN. CRITERIA: Location qualifies for IRS 30C credit	MIN. CRITERIA: Retail margins of at least $0.25/kWh
IF NOT: Seek other reimbursements	IF NOT: Consider adding solar + storage

All four elements of the Charging Profitability Matrix must be modeled together. For example, utilities that offer generous up-front incentive programs often impose crippling demand fees on your monthly bill, while utilities with low demand fees tend to instead impose high costs for energy (see chapter 3). And even winning a generous 80% NEVI infrastructure grant (see chapter 7) won't help you if the site is anticipated to have minimal charging activity, or if retail margins will be upside down from day one.

The Charging Profitability Matrix quadrants can be viewed as four legs of a chair. *You can break even if all four elements fall within the minimum criteria*, while the site will struggle to be profitable if any one of them is too far off the mark—unless counterbalanced by more attractive figures in other three quadrants. Note I chose the minimum criteria based on typical revenues and costs observed with sites having four chargers—such as required by the NEVI funding program.[1]

Once you are comfortable that the targeted site has promise, then suitable hardware and software can be selected, as described in chapters 5 and 6, and the steps described in chapter 9 can be implemented to ensure the site is built to be future-proofed, reliable, and productive.

Now, before going any further, let's address "the elephant in the room." *When it comes to building and operating fast-charging facilities, no one comes close to having the economies of scale of Tesla*. So whatever you install

---

1. In rough terms, over five years we have on the income side about $500,000 in margins: representing eight 35 kWh sessions per day at each of four chargers at $0.25 per kWh. On the expense side we have $200,000 to acquire and install the equipment after tax credits, and $300,000 in utility demand fees ($10 at 500kW/month).

will be significantly more expensive than a comparable facility built with Tesla's vertically-integrated supply chain. But even a company as dominant as Tesla can't install chargers everywhere they are needed. And, as this book goes to press in June of 2024, Tesla has made significant cuts to its staff and budgets for constructing additional charging stations. I would thus encourage you to study the principles outlined in here to see if your business can benefit from offering charging services to your employees and customers—even if it means little more than breaking even to benefit from increased customer attraction and foot traffic.

Also, when it comes to charging networks other than Tesla's, be aware that the pace of investment and acquisitions in the EV charging infrastructure space has been compared to a gold rush, where few have yet uncovered much in the way of gold.[2] Nevertheless, according to a recent data analysis by Stable Auto, utilization rates doubled last year, with every fast-charging cord in the country being used for an average of nearly five hours a day by the end of 2023. This surge indicates not just an increase in EV adoption but also a shift toward profitability for charging providers.[3]

I will close this brief introductory section by setting the stage for how the retail fast-charging infrastructure has evolved up to the present time. Until recently, there

---

2. https://evstation.com/charging-industry-mergers-acquisitions-deals/
3. https://stable.auto/insights/electric-vehicle-charger-utilization-by-month

have been three categories of early developers in this nascent market:[4]

- **automakers** such as Tesla and Volvo who need working chargers in the field to help them sell vehicles (even if it means losing money on the services);
- **Electrify America**, who is required to install chargers as part of parent-company Volkswagen's $14.7 billion settlement for cheating on diesel emissions testing; and
- **speculative charging networks** funded by public and private equity.

Now, here is were *you* come in. As EVs become more mainstream, a fourth category is emerging in the form of *retail business owners*, who are able to enhance profits by installing chargers in needed locations, while at the same time increasing foot traffic to their businesses. This book is written with you in mind.

---

4. An argument could be made that taxpayers and utility ratepayers represent another investor category, but I would suggest that such funding is common to all charging network operators.

BOOK NOTES

- In order to avoid bias and information obsolescence, where practical I have intentionally omitted references to specific companies, products, and services. Instead, I describe categories of market participants and how to identify them.

- I have provided over one hundred hyperlinks to additional information sources in both the body of the text and in footnotes for you to drill down on various topics. If these links are important to you, then the eBook version will be helpful. You can find the eBook at Amazon (Kindle app) or Apple (Books app).

- I wrote this book myself without any assistance by AI or computer learning systems. If you find errors, or just want to get in touch, please feel free to reach out using the contact form on my website: www.Objective.Energy.

CHAPTER 1

OUTSOURCE VS. OWN & OPERATE

> "When a person with money meets a person with experience . . . here is what happens: The person with the experience winds up with the money, and the person with the money winds up with the experience."
>
> — Harvey Mackay

Not long ago one of my business acquaintances called on an owner of a small truck stop that is located at a busy interstate freeway exit. A sales representative from an EV charging network had recently paid a visit to this truck stop owner to offer a ten-year lease agreement covering a potential half dozen EV charging stalls. The sales pitch included visions of increased convenience store traffic and subsidies via a supposed "partnering" arrangement this charging network had with the government—all wrapped up with time pressure to sign due to an impending funding program deadline. My jaw dropped as we reviewed the lopsided lease terms and conditions, which effectively provided the network operator with *exclusive rights* to offer charging at that location for *ten years*, in exchange for a few hundred bucks a year and some token profit-sharing. Worse, no payments would be made whatsoever until the network operator actually gets around to installing something. Fortunately, the truck stop owner didn't take the bait. But many do.

In contrast, a multistate retail store chain that I'm acquainted with has been providing property leases to competing charging networks for over the past half decade. Commercial terms include upfront fees, revenue-sharing, and reasonable cancellation clauses for nonperformance. Now that the retailer has some experience with *others* taking on the business risks of EV charging, they are beginning to install and operate their *own* chargers at locations, which are most likely to yield substantial returns on investment.

The point to be made here is that potential charging site providers must first consider if it makes financial sense to own and operate the facility, or if leasing parking stalls and real estate for someone else to own and operate is the better model?

There are significant trade-offs with each approach:

	Outsource to Others	Own and Operate
Restrictive covenants	Noncompete	None, other than those within incentive funding programs
Upside	Limited	Unlimited
Downside	Potential lost opportunity for nonperformance	CapEx (less incentives) Software fees

If your primary objective is to bring more foot traffic to a business, and you are of the opinion that EV adoption will be a long time in coming, then negotiating a fair deal with an established charging network is a compelling business model. You might as well let the other party bear most of the risk. On the other hand, outsourcing will leave money on the table if the site experiences high utilization. In the paragraphs below, and in chapter 8, some figures are provided around the potential return on investment (ROI) of owning and operating, but for now, here are some points to consider as you compare the two business models.

OUTSOURCED BUSINESS MODEL

If you decide to go with the outsourced model and let others own and operate the charging facility, then some of the commercial terms you will want to negotiate and document include the following.

EXCLUSIVITY AND PERFORMANCE

The network operator will be investing capital and resources into developing the site. This risk is customarily offset by some period of exclusive rights to operate EV charging at the location. On the other hand, a site host should have the contractual right to cancel if the operator doesn't get underway with building the charging facility within a specified period of time, or if charging availability uptime does not meet certain criteria once operational. It is not unusual to see exclusivity agreements of at least five years in duration, and up to ten years for larger sites. Pay special attention to assignability clauses, as the charging network space is ever evolving with associated mergers and acquisitions continually on the horizon.

LEASE FEES

Depending on the region, parking areas can be scarce, and not all stalls carry the same value. This is especially true for convenience stores, where significant revenue is derived from stalls located directly in front of the store, as compared with those located out beyond the fueling areas. At the current state of the art, a complete EV charging session requires anywhere from at least 20 minutes up to an hour, which could tie up premium stalls that would otherwise serve your quick in-and-out customers. The other aspect of lease fees is value placed on property occupied by the network operator's ancillary equipment, such as electrical switchgear, cabinets, and battery storage. Depending on the charging design, these items can sometimes be placed out of sight and far away from the chargers—with the trade-off of requiring additional up-front costs in cutting asphalt, trenching, and cable runs out to the chargers.

REVENUE SHARING

The traditional lease model includes property fees and revenue sharing. Revenue sharing is usually stated as either a percentage of sales or as cents per kWh delivered. Site hosts might also consider negotiating some degree of revenue sharing derived from other sources, such as the following:

- Connection fees, which are a one-time cost at the start of each session (typically up to $0.99).
- Idle fees, which are per-minute costs for remaining at a charger after the EV has reached 80% state of charge (these can be as high as $1 per minute).
- Advertising revenues, if the charger supports large screen displays.

Some network operators propose *profit sharing* rather than *revenue sharing*, but I'm not a fan of this approach; the way in which profits are calculated becomes a complicated point of negotiation, and applicable costs must be narrowly defined to avoid misunderstandings later on.

SITE ACCESS AND SECURITY

Revenue sharing aligns your interests with the charging network provider when it comes to site accessibility. Drivers expect to be able to charge around the clock, all year long, and no one is making money when the chargers are inaccessible. You will also need to work with the network operator to ensure the stalls are not encumbered by other vehicles, and that lighting and other physical security systems are in place and always operational.

OWN & OPERATE MODEL

The financial upside for owning and operating an EV charging facility can be attractive. But you must be mindful of the risks. Chapter 8 takes a deep dive on modeling return on investment, but for now I'm going to present a few simple, illustrative case studies using real-world, anonymized data.[1] *Some of the terminology and descriptions of equipment and utility rates will be unfamiliar to you at this point in the book.* But don't worry, you will become a pro at all of this by the time we are through!

SITE #1: ULTRAFAST 250 KW LARGE SITE—HIGH UTILIZATION

This is a twelve-stall facility offering charging speeds of up to 250 kW. It is located within a mile of a freeway off-ramp in a semirural community and averages *ten charges per stall per day*. The owner-operator enjoys economies of scale when it comes to equipment and overall build costs, as the subject site is one of many installed already. Although energy costs at this site are well below the national average, utility *demand fees* are a challenge at $15/kW. You will learn all about these fees in chapter 4; suffice it to say that use of cost mitigation strategies and battery buffering equipment, which I describe in chapter 5, provided the means to get utility demand down to an average of 80 kW per stall, yet the chargers can still deliver up to 250 kW to the vehicles. Retail pricing provides about $0.30 in gross margin per kWh dispensed, and the location also qualified for the IRS 30C tax credit. When taken altogether, this site meets three out of four criteria in our Profitability Matrix and is a successful project.

---

1. I've intentionally performed some aggressive rounding and estimating to preserve anonymity.

	Annual		Five Year
Revenues	$540,000	Cumulative Margins	$1,430,000
Energy & Utility	($236,000)	Build Cost after tax credit	($718,000)
Operating Expense	($18,000)	Cost of Capital	($135,000)
Gross Margins	**$286,000**	Cumulative Cashflow	**$577,000**

SITE #2: ULTRAFAST 300 KW
SMALL SITE—MEDIUM UTILIZATION

The next site to consider is a two-stall facility offering charging speeds above 300 kW, that also uses battery buffering to help mitigate demand fees. It is located at a convenience store within a mile of a very busy arterial off-ramp in a large urban area, and it averages *eight charges per stall per day*. Despite being in a relatively high utility cost region, the site has been able to maintain premium pricing as compared to slower charging offerings nearby. This provides about $0.24 in gross margin per kWh dispensed.

	Annual		Five Year
Revenues	$115,000	Cumulative Margins	$260,000
Energy & Utility	($59,000)	Build Cost	($110,000)
Operating Expense	($4,000)	Cost of Capital	($21,000)
Gross Margins	**$52,000**	Cumulative Cashflow	**$129,000**

The notable thing about this site is that the actual build cost was $210,000, but a grant program brought this down to $110,000. Were it not for the grant, the site would have essentially been a break-even scenario, as per the Profitability Matrix. Nevertheless, increase in store traffic has made this a profitable add-on to a traditional fueling and convenience store business.

SITE #3: SLOW MIDSIZE SITE—LOW UTILIZATION

Finally, let's take a look at an unfortunate situation where the site is averaging only *one charge per stall per day*. On the surface this seems odd, because it is ideally situated in the parking lot of a popular coffee store chain and only a couple of miles from a busy interstate freeway exit. But the first problem is that the four chargers have maximum charging speeds of only 62 kW. And the second problem is that a large ultrafast 250 kW charging facility was recently established even closer to the freeway. As a result, only those who really want to kill an hour or two over a venti caffè latte bother to stop here.

	Annual		Five Year
Revenues	$19,000	Cumulative Margins	$50,000
Energy & Utility	($7,000)	Build Cost	($170,000)
Operating Expense	($2,000)	Cost of Capital	($32,000)
Gross Margins	**$10,000**	**Cumulative Cashflow**	**($152,000)**

These real-world examples should help you understand why the subtitle of this book is *The Promises and Perils of Offering Electric Vehicle Charging Services*.

LESSONS LEARNED

As the owner of site #3 has painfully learned, pinching pennies upfront with low-cost, obsolete slow DC chargers can doom a site before the first shovel of earth is turned. Reflecting this, we are currently witnessing a "race to the bottom" when it comes to the pricing of slow DC chargers. A 50 kW so-called "DC fast charger" with two dispensing cables can be had for as little as $25,000 today—which is about one third the cost of acquiring a comparable 300 kW dual-port ultrafast charger. Unsuspecting site hosts often choose slow chargers for not only the low capital expense but also to avoid high up-front utility impact fees and other utility "make-ready" costs associated with faster dispensing equipment. Again, I detail these utility cost considerations in chapter 3.

Another lesson learned from the above examples is that economies of scale really do matter, and this is where the established charging networks shine. They may not share much of this value if you choose to outsource charging as the property owner, but it does allow them to make investments into locations that would otherwise be somewhat marginal. That being said, it is currently a buyer's market for EV chargers, with over 60 companies competing for your business. Please refer to chapter 5 for additional insight on equipment selection.

Last but not least, incentive funding can allow even small facilities to accelerate ROI, as is the case with site #2. I go into some detail into how to find such incentives in the next chapter.

CHAPTER 2

FINDING THE MONEY

> "The problem with socialism is that you eventually run out of other people's money."
> — Margaret Thatcher

There are billions of taxpayer and utility ratepayer dollars being invested today on EV charging infrastructure incentives, and chances are good that many of the sites you are targeting will qualify for reimbursement in one form or another. Whether or not these programs are good public policy is outside the scope of this book, but for the purposes of determining site profitability, here are tips on where to find potential sources of funding to offset your investment.

My favorite go-to resource for identifying incentive funding programs around the country is the US Department of Energy's Alternative Fuels Data Center, located at afdc.energy.gov, where you can see laws and incentives by state and then apply filters by fuel (EVs) and by utility.

After selecting the state in question, you should then look for links to local Clean Cities Coalitions, where additional information and resources can be obtained. If you are serious about installing EV charging, then I highly recommend you join your local Coalition, as these organizations are well-connected with not only the Department of Energy but also with the right people at local utilities, regulatory agencies, and government organizations. Coalition members have historically been operators of fleet vehicles who are striving to replace petroleum use with alternative fuels. As you participate in the Coalition, you may get acquainted with others who are in need of EV charging along delivery or rideshare routes where your sites could be a good fit for regular charging sessions. You will also be one of the first to learn of new funding programs as they become available. Membership and participation in your local Clean Cities Coalition is money and time well spent.

In addition to the DOE's Alternative Fuels Data Center, the US Department of Transportation also provides a list of federal funding programs,[1] as does the DOT-DOE Joint Office of Energy and Transportation.[2] Another useful list of federal and state-by-state incentives is regularly posted at the website of EV charging network provider ChargePoint.[3] Finally, the Electrification Coalition also provides resources for identifying incentive programs.[4]

---

1. https://www.transportation.gov/rural/ev/toolkit/ev-infrastructure-funding-and-financing/federal-funding-programs
2. https://driveelectric.gov/resources
3. https://www.chargepoint.com/incentives
4. https://electrificationcoalition.org/ev-funding-finder/

Incentive programs generally fall into one of three categories:

1. tax credits,
2. utility reimbursements, and
3. government grants.

To illustrate, I will provide current examples of each incentive category, realizing that by the time you read this the specific programs discussed may have become obsolete. However, the principles shared are common to most any program within each category.

TAX CREDITS

When it comes to qualifying for incentive funding, the easiest way to obtain reimbursement assistance is with tax credits offered on the federal, and sometimes state, levels. Unlike the other two incentive categories listed above, tax credits do not require preapproval nor are they awarded via a competitive RFP process. Simply put: if you qualify, you qualify. Tax credit programs are always subject to sunset dates, after which they must either be renewed by Congress or by the individual state that offers them.

You will need to consult with your accountant to ensure the applicable forms are completed on time, and be prepared if the credit is questioned in an audit. I know this seems easy, but as they say, "the devil is in the details."

Our first consideration is that EV infrastructure tax credits are almost always provided in the form of a *non-refundable* general business credit. This means that the entity claiming the incentive must have offsetting tax liability from which to claim the credit. Another consideration is if the tax liability is of a type for which the credit may be applied, and if any excess can be carried back or forward to other tax years. That being said, the Alternative Fuel Vehicle Refueling Property Credit I describe next can alternatively be claimed through *elective pay* (often called *direct pay*), meaning that governments and tax-exempt organizations can also benefit by selling or transferring the credits to others.[5]

ALTERNATIVE FUEL VEHICLE REFUELING PROPERTY CREDIT

The Alternative Fuel Vehicle Refueling Property Credit,[6] also known as the "30C credit," was greatly expanded in January 2024 and is an example of a federal tax incentive available at the time I am writing this. Business may claim up to 30% "per single item of qualified alternative fuel vehicle refueling property" up to $100,000 per item.[7] This is widely being interpreted as up to $30,000 in tax credits for each $100,000 or higher-cost DC fast charger placed in service during the tax year. The facility must remain operational for three full years or risk the IRS clawing back the credit.

There are some limitations to the 30C credit. Among them are requirements to use prevailing wage and apprenticeships, and that the property must be placed in service within low-income communities or within nonurban census tracts. You will want to seek professional advice

---

5. https://home.treasury.gov/news/press-releases/jy2035
6. https://www.irs.gov/credits-deductions/alternative-fuel-vehicle-refueling-property-credit
7. https://www.irs.gov/pub/irs-drop/n-24-20.pdf

on these requirements, but for now here are resources for a first-pass to see if the locations you are targeting might qualify:

- Argonne National Labs 30C Tax Credit Eligibility Locator map.[8]
- Formal Notice 2024-20 from the IRS.[9]

One geographical and time-sensitive limitation that I want to particularly note is Section 5, placed toward the end of IRS publication 2024-20. Here we learn that *2015 census tract boundaries will no longer be applicable after January 1, 2025.* As I look around the three layers provided in the sidebar of the Argonne Labs mapping tool, it is evident that this old census data covers wide swaths of the country, including areas that one would be hard-pressed to consider nonurban or low-income today. If your charging facility is reliant on "2011-2015 NMTC tracts" for 30C tax relief, then you had better get moving with your project soon!

STATE TAX CREDITS

Some states also provide income tax credits for clean fuel projects. For example, Oklahoma's Credit for Investment in Clean-Burning Motor Vehicle Fuel Property[10] is one of the most generous offerings in the country, providing up to 45% of the cost of installing commercial alternative fueling infrastructure, including EV charging. Again,

---

8. https://www.anl.gov/esia/refueling-infrastructure-tax-credit
9. https://www.irs.gov/pub/irs-drop/n-24-20.pdf
10. https://oklahoma.gov/content/dam/ok/en/tax/documents/forms/tax-credits/567-A.pdf

check with your local Clean Cities Coalition to see what tax credits might be available in your state.

OTHER CREDITS

You will also want to visit with your accountant about Investment Tax Credits and Production Tax Credits if the charging facility will include battery storage and/or solar production.[11]

UTILITY REIMBURSEMENTS

There are almost always some utility "make-ready" costs associated with preparing an EV charging site, such as transformer upgrades and additional power lines. The good news is that many utilities have been approved to have the general rate base cover some or all of these costs. When it comes to make-ready incentive programs, each utility will delineate the degree of assistance provided to the site owner. Many utilities will assist on the utility side of the meter, but some are even more generous. Below is an example from PSEG Long Island, where not only the utility side is eligible but the customer side as well—all the way up to the EV charger.[12]

Some utility programs provide partial reimbursement for the EV charger too, often predicated on somewhat cumbersome approved lists of charger makes and models.[13] Eversource Connecticut provides an extreme

---

11. https://www.energy.gov/eere/solar/federal-solar-tax-credits-businesses
12. https://www.psegliny.com/en/saveenergyandmoney/GreenEnergy/EV/MakeReady
13. https://briteswitch.com/news/hassle-of-approved-lists-for-ev-charger-rebates.php

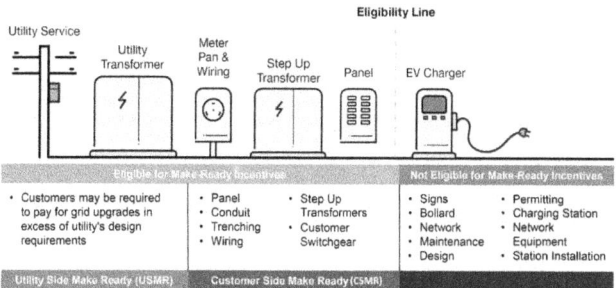

Image courtesy of PSEG Long Island

example of generous rebate funding, where under a recent program sites were eligible for not only 100% reimbursements of make-ready costs but also 50% reimbursements for the EV charging hardware—up to a whopping $250,000 per site.[14]

Now, before we get too carried away in praising the generosity of utilities and their ratepayers, there is a "no free lunch" observation to be made here. By and large, *those utilities that provide the most generous upfront incentives are often ones with relatively high rates for energy and power demand.* We will discuss utility rates in chapter 4; suffice it to say that when it comes to site selection, beware of overly focusing on up-front incentives alone. You must weigh in the balance all four elements of the Charging Profitability Matrix described in the introduction of this book.

---

14. https://portal.ct.gov/-/media/PURA/EV-Charging-Program-Manual.pdf

GOVERNMENT GRANTS

As I write this, the US federal government is well underway with implementing the $7.5 billion National Electric Vehicle Infrastructure (NEVI) Formula Program. As NEVI is such a significant aspect of EV infrastructure initiatives today, I have dedicated chapter 7 entirely to this topic.

Generally speaking, government grants are limited in scope to certain geographic regions and communities. Some cost-matching by the participant is also required.

Commonly targeted categories of funding for EV infrastructure include the following:

- Workplaces
- Tourism areas
- Rural and underserved communities
- Multiunit dwellings

EV infrastructure grant programs often require that

- the site must be networked with a reputable backend software provider, which I discuss in chapter 6;
- equipment must be listed with a nationally recognized testing laboratory;
- charging must be made available to the general public, either 24/7 or at least during normal business hours;
- transactions must not require membership or unique payment methods; and
- reporting must to be provided to the funding source at regular intervals as to facility uptime, along with anonymized charging session history.

CLEAN FUEL STANDARD CREDITS

In addition to tax credits, utility incentives, and government grants, you may also be eligible to accrue valuable credits for energy dispensed if your site is in a state that has adopted a Clean Fuel Standard. California pioneered this type of incentive under its Low Carbon Fuel Standard (LCFS) program.[15] Washington, Oregon, and New Mexico have adopted similar regulations, and legislatures in Hawaii, Illinois, Michigan, New Jersey, and New York have active bills under consideration.

In a nutshell, these programs require the aggregate carbon intensity of all vehicle fuel dispensed in the state to not exceed ever-stringent annual thresholds. So if you are dispensing a high-carbon fuel (such as gasoline), you are going to have to purchase credits from someone who is dispensing low-carbon fuels (such as electricity

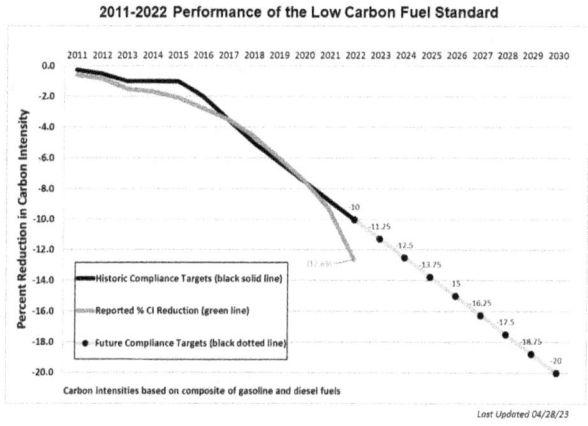

California LCFS Dashboard

---

15. https://ww2.arb.ca.gov/our-work/programs/low-carbon-fuel-standard

sourced from renewables) in order to remain compliant. This can be viewed as a hidden carbon tax, and it is part of the reason why California motorists pay some of the highest prices in the nation for gasoline.

Clean Fuel credits can add up for an EV charging station site host. For example, due to increased generation of renewable energy in California, the LCFS program currently sets the carbon intensity of EV charging off the California grid as being about 83% of gasoline's carbon intensity.[16] And, as of 2024, anyone who is dispensing vehicle fuel there is subject to meeting a 12% reduction in carbon vis-a-vis gasoline.[17] So California EV charging facilities are compliant now by simply charging off the grid, and they will likely remain so as California's grid continues to add renewable energy sources. But when you consider that solar energy is counted as a zero-carbon fuel, adding solar collection to your site will yield LCFS credits that can be monetized—especially if there are also batteries to store and deliver the renewable energy into EVs when the sun isn't shining (or the wind isn't blowing if you install wind generation). And when it comes to solar with battery storage, California provides the opportunity to "double dip" by layering state incentives such as the California Self Generation Incentive Program[18] onto federal tax credits.

Clean Fuel regulations and renewable energy credits can be complex, and although I have placed this discussion in the "Finding the Money" chapter, be advised that

---

16. https://ww2.arb.ca.gov/sites/default/files/classic/fuels/lcfs/fuelpathways/comments/tier2/elec_update.pdf
17. https://ww2.arb.ca.gov/resources/documents/lcfs-data-dashboard
18. https://www.cpuc.ca.gov/industries-and-topics/electrical-energy/demand-side-management/self-generation-incentive-program

this is indeed a two-edged sword. If your state has a Clean Fuels regulation and fossil fuels are the primary source of grid electricity, then you may find yourself having to *purchase* credits as opposed to being able to *monetize* them. I would encourage you to take a close look at Clean Fuels regulations if your state is one of those that have adopted, or are now adopting, such standards.

CHAPTER 3

SITE SELECTION

"The three most important factors in determining the desirability of a property are 'location, location, location.'"

— Harold Samuel

Unlike traditional fuels, the deck is stacked against making a business case for investing in public EV charging. While owners of gasoline and diesel vehicles have no choice but to pull into a fuel stop, according to the DOE some 80% of EV charging is done at home.[1] This percentage will decline somewhat as EV adoption makes its way toward more car owners who do not have reliable off-street parking. Meanwhile, determining which locations fill a need for the remaining one-in-five charging sessions is no simple task.

Site selection encompasses all of the Charging Profitability Matrix elements provided in the introduction of

---

1. https://www.nrel.gov/docs/fy21osti/78540.pdf

this book. It is a determining factor in potential charging volume, potential reimbursements, and utility rate schedules. But before getting to these important topics, I will first address *site feasibility*.

HIGH VOLTAGE POWER AVAILABILITY

You may have chosen a location where EV drivers are lining up to empty their wallets, but the site will never dispense a single electron without a robust grid connection to supply it. With the exception of certain battery-buffered systems (which I describe in chapter 5), DC fast chargers almost universally require *three-phase 480 volt* grid supply to power them. This is the "secondary" service supplied to utility customers who need significant power to run large buildings or industrial equipment. The utility provides this by transforming down higher voltage "primary" (or "high-tension") service, which is usually supplied at 12,470 volts or higher from power poles or underground conduits.

Before reaching out to the electric utility, I would invite you to first check the as-built engineering drawings, along with looking around each target property (including adjacent properties) to see if there are transformers, circuit breaker panels, or meters that indicate the presence of 480 volt power on or nearby the

Marking on 480 V transformer

Transformer sticker indicating 12,470 V primary service, up to 225 kVa current site. The photos here will give you a sense of what to look for. Selecting a site that already has 480 volt service gets you into the game quickly. Utilities often plan ahead for additional load, and you may find there is spare capacity already at the transformer to provide for at least one 150 kW or faster charger (or many chargers if they feature integrated battery buffering).

Unfortunately, the vast majority of businesses who are looking to install DC fast chargers—such as convenience stores, restaurants, and auto dealerships—are instead equipped with *three-phase 208 volt* service. While this isn't necessarily a showstopper, it does delay things, and it adds to utility make-ready costs. The utility will have to upgrade service by way of one or more of the following—in decreasing order of desirability:

- A "pole drop" if there are wires above ground with capacity to supply 480 volts. This is an ideal scenario, as it requires minimal time and expense. But it can sometimes be limited in scalability.

- A transformer replacement. This is an option when the existing 208 volt transformer is connected to primary, high-voltage service, which is often the case. Replacing it with a 480 volt transformer is a relatively straightforward job. Note, however, that

480 volt "pole drop"

lead times on new 480 volt transformers are currently more than one year in many parts of the country.

- A "buck-boost" transformer, which transforms 208 volts up to 480 volts. This is an option only if the existing 208 volt service has ample spare capacity.
- An expensive and time-consuming project to bring high-voltage primary service to a location on or nearby the site, and then transforming this down to 480 volts. Expect to pay at least $50,000 in make-ready and impact fees, and hope that your utility provides infrastructure rebate programs for EV charging facilities as described in chapter 2.

SPARE CAPACITY

Once you have narrowed down the candidate sites to those with existing or readily-available 480 volt service, the next step in a feasibility study is to determine spare capacity. This is done by first determining the maximum power that can be drawn from the transformer, and then comparing this figure to the maximum demand that the site requires from the grid any given time. Note that power is expressed as kilowatts (kW) or kilovolt-amperes (kVa), and these terms are often used interchangeably—albeit it takes around 1.2 kVa to equal one kW.

In the photo earlier in this chapter we note the sticker on the transformer indicates "0225 kVa," which tells us that this transformer is capable of providing up to 225 kVa, or about *190 kW* of power at 480 V. Assuming this transformer is not being shared by other facilities, we can then look at our utility bills to see the maximum one-time demand drawn on this transformer over the course of a year. In the adjacent bill excerpt we see that this was *101.8 kW*. Our spare capacity is thus approximately *88 kW*. In this scenario, the utility would probably approve the installation of one 50 kW charger without having to perform a load study and/or upgrade the transformer.

Utility bill indicating maximum annual demand

34,610	kWh used
1,153.7	Daily avg hWh
1,276.9	Daily avg kWh last month
↓5.5%	Change in daily avg kWh from last year
↓9.7%	Change in daily avg kWh from last month
86.9	Max monthly demand
101.8	Max annual demand
30↻	Days in billing cycle

Of course, new vehicle owners today are looking for at least 150 kW charging speeds as they travel. So our hypothetical charging site could begin with offering an inexpensive 50 kW charger (there are many reliable models out there for under $25,000) while waiting on a utility upgrade for the eventual high-speed, multiple charger offering. The charging site could also consider use of on-site battery buffering, which could potentially allow for much faster charging speeds off the limited 50 kW grid feed. I discuss battery-buffered charging in some detail in chapter 5.

Last but certainly not least, you need to consider where the proposed site is located in relationship to core grid infrastructure. It is no coincidence that many charging facilities built and operated by the established

EV charging networks are located either next to utility power substations; below high-capacity, high-voltage power lines; or within industrial and manufacturing regions. This is because the farther you get from core "primary service" electrical infrastructure, the less likely the utility will be able to serve you with the power needed. Sites on the fringe also tend to be hit with higher impact fees and can suffer from "harmonics" in the lines and higher-than-normal voltage peaks and dips. Work with your utility to determine where 480 volt power can be made available at a reasonable cost, and at the scale required for your peak charging loads.

POTENTIAL CHARGING VOLUME

Now that you have determined site feasibility from the perspective of utility power supply, the next consideration is potential demand for the charging services. Getting back to the Charging Profitability Matrix provided in the introduction, owning and operating generally makes sense if you are anticipating an average of *eight or more charges per day, per stall*, over the investment time horizon. Determining if this hurdle can be met is challenging, because it requires some degree of geospatial data analytics along with following your "gut" feelings on the opportunity.

In determining potential charging volume, we will consider the three broad categories of public charging consumers:

1. EV owners who live in the region,
2. travelers who must charge during trips that exceed the vehicle's range, and
3. operators of EV fleets.

1. DATA ON REGIONAL EV OWNERSHIP

As noted above, because most charging is done at home or the workplace, the mere fact that there are many EVs registered in the area doesn't necessarily mean these owners are frequenting public chargers. That being said, all EV drivers occasionally need to charge somewhere to get home safely from a trip that exceeds vehicle range (in other words, it's not so much about getting *from Point A to Point B*, but rather it's about getting *from Point B back to Point A*). Also, roughly 40% of US households don't have convenient access to EV charging overnight where they live either.[2] So knowing where the vehicles are concentrated is a good first step to determining potential charging volumes.

Here are some resources to help you determine the concentration of EV owners in a given geographical area.

- **The Open Vehicle Registration Initiative**[3] is a free data resource on EV registrations by zip code, make, and model. The site provides CSV (spreadsheet) downloads of this data for further analysis. There are currently 17 states participating in this program, including those with high rates of EV adoption such as CA, CO, FL, NJ, NY, TX, and WA.

- **Consulting firm EVAdoption**[4] provides commercial reports on EV sales by state, and other reports on charging infrastructure deployments.

---

2. https://evadoption.com/parking-evs-in-driveways-and-on-the-street-implications-for-ev-charging/
3. https://www.atlasevhub.com/materials/state-ev-registration-data/
4. https://evadoption.com/reports/

- **The Alternative Fuels Data Center** maintains a free database of vehicle counts by state, albeit somewhat dated as this book goes to print.[5]
- **The EPRI eRoadMAP**[6] is a free resource directed at utility planners to estimate the amount of energy needed at a local level to electrify transportation. This is a terrific free planning tool for EV charging site hosts because it takes into account the Department of Energy's county-level EV adoption forecasts, along with statewide zero-emission vehicle regulations and real-world data from Amazon and other stakeholders.

2. DATA ON TRAVELING EVs

There are a number of emerging geospatial data analytics companies that attempt to estimate potential charger utilization. The demonstrations are impressive: you enter in an address, along with the number of planned chargers, and out pops a report spanning the next ten years. They all operate on the same premise: that AI and machine learning can estimate anticipated charger activity by combining public and proprietary databases on EV ownership, nearby charger utilization, traffic patterns, demographics, amenities, etc. I've been evaluating a few of these offerings and have found that while some take the approach of keeping the underlying data proprietary (charging by the report), others offer a subscription fee with unlimited open access to data in geographies of

---

5. https://afdc.energy.gov/vehicle-registration
6. https://eroadmap.epri.com/

interest—and from there you can come up with your own conclusions.

Since many of my clients already have subscriptions to customer and geographic database services, our approach is to first leverage these resources to help identify promising sites for traveling consumers generally, look at EV penetration in the region, and then perform some old-school investigative techniques to validate if a given site will draw the needed charging business. Sometimes this means simply reading the utility meters at existing fast-charging facilities over time to quantify the volume of business being discharged in the region, and observing when EVs tend to queue up at sites where demand exceeds the supply of charging stalls, etc. Once we have done what we can with existing information, subscribing to one of the EV-centric geospatial analysis tools can provide validation prior to making the investment.

3. OPERATORS OF EV FLEETS

Seek to identify fleet operators with whom you can contract for charging services. Examples include rideshare, delivery van pools, and the emerging medium- and heavy-duty vehicle segment. As described in the previous chapter, membership in Clean Cities Coalitions is a good first step in getting acquainted with these fleet operators.

REASONABLE UTILITY RATES

As you consider site selection, it is imperative to know what rate schedules may apply to each site, as this will have a significant effect on ROI. I have on occasion consulted with potential site hosts who thought they were ready to go ahead with an EV charging project due to attractive grants, incentives, and potential charging traffic—only to discover that the applicable utility rate structure would doom any hope of profitability.

Deciphering utility rates can be so perplexing that I've devoted the next chapter entirely to this topic. Also, chapter 8 provides a deep-dive on how to calculate ROI, where utility rates play a significant part in the modeling.

OTHER FEASIBILITY CONSIDERATIONS

Of course, site preparation and construction will cost less at undeveloped properties and at locations that can combine the charger installation with other planned construction activities, such as addition of lighting. You should also discuss with your design engineering group if there are potential roadblocks associated with the targeted site, such as

- propensity for flooding;
- how the chargers might affect traffic patterns;
- if at least one pull-through charger could be offered;
- utility and other right-of-ways;
- code requirements to separate chargers from gas pumps, vent stacks;
- limitations on trenching, cutting asphalt, etc.

CHAPTER 4

GETTING A GRIP ON UTILITY RATES

"After potential charging traffic, utility rate structure is the foremost consideration in deciding where to place an EV charging facility, what equipment to place there, or if the investment is even worth considering."

For over a century, we have become accustomed to producing, storing, and delivering vehicle fuel as we would almost any physical good. Energy producers are able to turn up petroleum wells, refine, store, and deliver gasoline or diesel whenever and wherever the demand exists. This energy-dense stuff is easily transported over pipelines and roads and is mostly subject to free market economics. However, the production and delivery game completely changes when it comes to EV charging.

It is no trivial task for an electric utility to plan around serving a new fast-charging facility within their territory. This is because when it comes to reliably supplying electrical loads, energy must be *produced* and *delivered* in *real-time*,[1] and firing up one 250 kW DC fast charger is similar to having 50 suburban homes suddenly turning on their central air conditioners all at once! It's the random nature of these grid-impacting charging events that causes heartburn for utility planners and grid operators, and why the traditional utility rate structure is understandably detrimental to charging ROI.

Utilities are, by nature, monopoly enterprises. There are over 3,000 of them in the United States,[2] and they fall into three categories:

- **Investor-owned utilities** are typically large enterprises that are traded on a public stock exchange. Sometimes referred to as "IOUs," they are regulated by each state in which they operate. Almost three-quarters of utility customers get their electricity from these companies.[3]

- **Utility cooperatives** are not-for-profit, owned by the ratepayers whom they serve, and are commonly located in rural areas of the country. As with IOUs, "Co-ops" are also regulated by each state in which they operate.

- **Publicly owned utilities** are owned by a government entity or political subdivision, such as a city or municipality. They function as a public service of the entity and are regulated by its governing body, such as a city council.

---

1. Use of on-site battery buffers for EV charging can overcome some of this challenge, which I will discuss in more detail in chapter 5.
2. https://www.eia.gov/todayinenergy/detail.php?id=40913
3. Ibid.

You will find that most utilities are happy to advise you as to the feasibility of a proposed charging facility project and will provide realistic costs and timelines for serving the power needed. But you should also bear in mind that the vast majority of utility-provided EV infrastructure incentive programs are provided by IOUs, as they tend to be more more involved in shaping state legislative policies.

No matter the category, utilities all have geographical service boundaries and are required to publish a rate tariff with associated schedules. These tariffs and schedules can be intimidating, often filling hundreds of pages. But as a charging site host, you have got to understand them. Because after potential charging traffic, utility rate structure is the foremost consideration in deciding where to site an EV charging facility, what equipment to place there, or if the investment is even worth considering.

ENERGY FEES AND DEMAND FEES

Utility bills and rate schedules include a number of line items, but there are two core elements that really matter when it comes to the ROI on EV charging:

- **power consumption** (expressed in **kWh**), and
- **power demand** (expressed in **kW**).

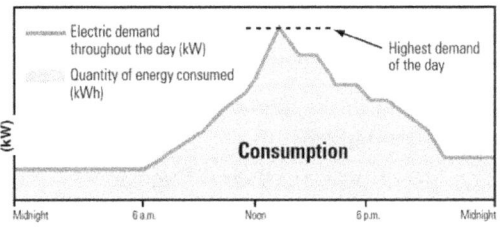

Image courtesy of We Energies

POWER CONSUMPTION (kWh)

Power consumption is a relatively easy concept to grasp. To help you visualize this, think of consumption as electrons flowing through a cable, with a meter spinning around to measure how many electrons flow past the meter over a given period of time. Power consumption is expressed in kilowatt-hours (kWh)—a classic example of this being the energy consumed should ten 100 watt light bulbs be lit for an hour (10 x 100 watts = 1 kW of energy flowing over the space of one hour, or 1 kWh). Note that in the previous graph the meter was spinning much faster at noon than it it was at midnight, but for the purposes of calculating power consumption, we don't care about the *speed* of the meter spinning around but of the *quantity* the meter observes during a billing cycle (i.e., the volume of gray area in the graph). Pricing for this power consumed is always shown on a rate schedule or on a monthly invoice as $/kWh.

POWER DEMAND (kW)

Power demand, on the other hand, is indeed all about the top *speed* of the meter spinning around as observed during a billing cycle. This maximum speed is indicated by the dashed line on the previous graph. You see, the faster the meter spins at any given time, the more strain is placed on the grid to keep up with this increased demand for energy, and the more cost a utility must bear to be ready for such a spike in demand.

Put another way, if the graph represented *water demand* rather than *electricity demand*, the water utility would be installing a *fire hydrant* on the property rather than a *garden hose spigot* so as to prepare for the noon gusher—even though this fixture would be overkill at midnight when a garden hose spigot would otherwise suffice. To carry the analogy further, the water utility must also place large-diameter pipes in the ground and build a water tower somewhere nearby to have capacity ready at a moment's notice to satisfy this need for sudden water flow. So who pays for all of this unusual infrastructure? (Hint: it's not the guy next door who only requires a garden hose spigot.)

In summary, power demand charges (hereafter referred to as *demand fees*) are calculated by looking back over the billing cycle to determine the highest kW strain placed on the grid, and then multiplying this figure by a regulated rate schedule price expressed as $/kW. As we will see next, managing this element of your monthly bill is paramount when it comes to EV charging!

A TALE OF TWO CHARGING FACILITIES

Let's consider a published rate structure in New York City,[4] where the utility is approved to offer *energy* at $0.09 per kWh, and to offer *demand* at $33 per kW.[5] Now let's assume there are two EV charging facilities in the Big Apple, each tasked with charging up vehicles with 50 kWh of energy per charging session.

---

4. https://lite.coned.com/_external/cerates/documents/elecPSC10/electric-tariff.pdf
5. Weighted average for new accounts under ConEd's schedule SC-9 Rate I as of March 16, 2024.

- Site #1 has a single **10 kW** Level 2 AC charger (think of this as a garden hose spigot in the water analogy), which slowly charges a few delivery vans whenever they are sitting idle. It takes about *five hours* (50 kWh battery / 10 kW speed) to charge up each van. But that's okay because no one is driving them overnight anyway.

- Site #2 has a single **200 kW** DC fast charger (think of this as a fire hydrant in the water analogy) to rapidly charge the taxis and ride-sharing fleet. It only takes *15 minutes* (50 kWh battery / 200 kW speed) to charge up each EV.[6] High-speed charging is necessary in this use case because a driver sitting around waiting for a slow Level 2 charge isn't making any money, and the cars are in service around the clock.

If both sites experience 100 charging sessions during a billing cycle, the utility will bill these sites the same for *energy consumed*, based on $0.09 per kWh.

	Delivery Vans	**Taxis**
Dispensed (100 x 50 kWh)	5,000	5,000
Energy Rate (kWh)	$0.09	$0.09
Cost of Power	**$450**	**$450**

---

6. Of course, no EV currently on the market can charge at a continuous 200 kW rate (although some come close to this on average), but for this simple example we ignore vehicle charging curves.

So far, so good. But now we turn to the cost of *demand*:

	Delivery Vans	Taxis
Peak Demand (kW)	10	200
Demand Rate (kW)	$33	$33
Cost of Demand	**$330**	**$6,600**

As we see, the fast-charging site must pay over *$6,000 more per month* if the utility is to deliver 200 kW on demand. Perhaps this is money well spent—such as in our example of a taxi and ride-sharing fleet where downtime can mean lost revenue. But now imagine if there were four chargers,[7] and that at some point in the billing cycle all of them were simultaneously charging EVs. Clearly even the most profitable ride-sharing service would have a hard time penciling out $25,000 in extra monthly utility costs to provide such an offering!

Now to be fair, New York City's $33 per kW demand rate is one of the highest in the country—and for good reason when you consider the challenge of maintaining and expanding a densely urban power grid that was originally designed and built over a century ago. Recognizing this, the New York Department of Public Service recently approved a temporary program to provide demand fee relief to EV charging facility customers by way of a monthly rebate, and more permanent rate structures are under consideration that will provide phase-in

---

7. Four chargers providing a minimum of 150 kW DC output is becoming a common metric, as this is the minimum site capability required under the federal National EV Infrastructure funding program (NEVI), as described in chapter 7.

demand fees based on load factors. So I'm not picking on Con Edison (nor on any other utility mentioned in this book); suffice it to say that most utility demand fees I have worked with around the country are priced between $5 and $15 per kW. But the key takeaway is that fast-charging facilities generally face significant ROI headwinds, especially if there is minimal charging activity at the site. In the above example, the first taxi to charge up at 200 kW speed triggers the $6,600 demand fee, which is owed even if no additional charging activity occurs during the billing cycle.

In summary, whenever you have a scenario where EVs are parking for extended periods of time (i.e., at hotels, entertainment venues, office parks, or at a fleet yard), installing Level 2 AC charging or low-cost slow 50 kW DC charging equipment is almost always a better option versus putting in ultrafast DC fast charging. Not only does this reduce demand fees but it also significantly lowers equipment installation and utility make-ready costs in the first place. Slow charging is also much gentler on the electric vehicle's battery health and longevity, and there are many owners of plug-in electric hybrid vehicles who seek Level 2 chargers while dining and staying overnight, too. See chapter 10 for additional advice on planning for Level 2 AC charging.

SPECIAL EV CHARGING RATES

Public utility regulators are recognizing that high demand fees cause a chilling effect on fast-charging investment, especially in these early years of EV adoption where there isn't much business yet to spread across the monthly demand fee. In response, some utilities have been approved to offer optional rate schedules (a.k.a. *rate riders*) that reduce or eliminate demand fees, with the trade-off of requiring higher energy fees instead. I provide an ROI analysis of one such schedule in chapter 8, where an approximate $16 demand fee can optionally be lowered to zero in exchange for an increase of about $0.17 per kWh in energy costs. Put another way, these optional rates trade-off demand fees for slimmer sales margins on energy dispensed. And as you will see in chapter 8, as volumes increase there comes a point when it is more advantageous to go back to the traditional demand rate schedule.

Some utilities take this concept to a granular level, offering a sliding-scale schedule for fast-charging sites, where the demand fees phase into normal as the site gains more activity (a.k.a. *load factor*). Here is an example from Connecticut's Eversource Energy:[8]

Load Factor	0-5%	5-10%	10-15%	15-20%	20-25%	25-30%	30-35%	>35%
Demand (kW)	0	$2.50	$5.00	$7.50	$10.00	$12.50	$15.00	$17.50
Energy (kWh)	$0.21	$0.20	$0.19	$0.18	$0.18	$0.17	$0.16	$0.15

The rationale behind load factor–based rate schedules is that charging facilities should be able to pay their fair share of demand charges once EV adoption increases. In the meantime, they contribute toward the rate base by paying more for energy consumed than would other commercial customers.

---

8. Figures are rounded. https://www.eversource.com/content/docs/rates-tariffs/ct-electric/rate-ev-l.pdf

TIME-OF-USE RATES

Things get a little more complex with Time-Of-Use (TOU) rate schedules. These schedules are often required for commercial customers, and they reflect the cost a utility must bear for reliably generating, buying, and delivering wholesale power when demand is greatest. The ROI analysis in chapter 8 includes a TOU rate schedule.

Alongside variable pricing for energy (kWh), some utilities also require variable pricing for demand (kW). Variable demand costs are sometimes listed on a rate schedule or invoice as *Peak Load Contribution*. Taken together, the energy and demand costs incurred by offering fast charging during peak hours is something to take seriously in a financial model. Most TOU rate schedules reflect high costs during weekday afternoons—which is probably not much of a concern if the site is anticipated to mostly serve travelers during weekends and holidays, but it could be a deal-breaker when planning a site that caters to commuter traffic. Many TOU schedules reflect higher costs during summer months, too.

Many public-access EV charging facilities are responding to variable rate schedules by including TOU pricing at the charger. But this is easier said than done, and implementing TOU rates for EV charging requires some additional planning. One consideration is if your back-end software and payments processing providers are able to implement TOU, and if the charging hardware can support dynamic pricing display. Another requirement to keep in mind is that

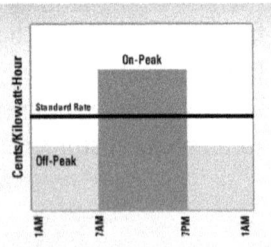

Image courtesy of We Energies

dynamic rate implementation must meet requirements of NIST 44 (weights and measures) whereby the rate must not change during the session. I provide more detail on NIST regulations in chapter 5.

YOU MIGHT HAVE TWO UTILITIES

In some markets, such as Texas and certain Northeast regions, you might find yourself working with two utilities: one *regulated distributor* of energy and another *unregulated producer* of energy. The premise is that transmission wires in the air and under the ground are necessarily owned and operated by a regulated monopoly, but you can separately choose from whom you buy power generation. If you are in one of these markets, then you will need to consider the rate structures of the regulated distribution utility alongside market pricing for energy in the region. Although you can't do anything about the former, you might find attractive options for the latter, especially when it comes to potentially trading off higher energy costs in exchange for lower demand fees associated with power generation.

UTILITY-OWNED CHARGERS

Our discussion of utility rates wouldn't be complete without touching on the controversial subject of rate schedules *that the utility itself follows* when offering charging services to the public. By way of background, in the early days of EV adoption, it was not uncommon for utilities to foster demand for electric vehicles by placing Level 2 and DC fast-charging facilities within their service areas. Such utility-led initiatives have mostly tapered off as for-profit entities have entered into the charging market, and public utility regulators along with consumer advocates have soured on use of ratepayer funds for this purpose.[9] Nevertheless, if your utility is one of the few that continue to offer public charging, it would behoove you to review the regulated rates at which they offer these services. You may find that pricing at utility-owned chargers is subsidized, rendering nearby facilities such as you are considering to be uncompetitive.[10]

ON-SITE POWER GENERATION

As you will recall, the Charging Profitability Matrix presented in the introduction of this book indicates that charger prices ought to at least provide $0.25/kW in retail margins. This can be difficult to achieve if you are in an area of the country that suffers from high electricity costs. If your utility rate schedules won't accommodate retail margins such as these, consider adding renewable energy generation from solar or wind alongside battery storage to help overcome this challenge on profitability. You may find that investment tax credits for renewables

---

9. See Charge Ahead Partnership, which is an alliance of public charging site hosts who oppose utility owned and operated charging facilities. https://www.chargeaheadpartnership.com/
10. For example: Florida Power and Light is approved to offer below-market rates of $0.30/kWh through 2025. https://www.fpl.com/content/dam/fplgp/us/en/rates/pdf/electric-tariff-section8.pdf. See also Rocky Mountain Power, with fast charging subsidized to as low as $0.22/kWh. https://www.rockymountainpower.net/content/dam/pcorp/documents/en/rockymountainpower/rates-regulation/utah/rates/060_Company_Operated_Electric_Vehicle_Charging_Station_Service.pdf

and storage provide enough offset to make this pencil out.

Oh, and don't forget your *other* energy utility. Use of fossil and/or renewable natural gas (RNG) to supplement renewable power generation on-site could be an attractive way to overcome high electric rates and constrained grid obstacles. I have found that in some scenarios the ROI can be compelling when compared against grid power alone. This is especially true in states that have Clean Fuel Standard Credit programs, such as described in chapter 2, because EV drivetrains are far more efficient than their RNG vehicle counterparts. And the negative carbon intensity of RNG can effectively triple Clean Fuel Standard credits earned as compared to charging EVs from the local grid.

ENERGY SERVICE COMPANIES (ESCOs)

Additional help with strategies to overcome high utility costs may be found by contracting with a reputable energy service company. The DOE maintains a list of qualified firms, who typically use the performance-based contracting methodology. When an ESCO implements a project, the company's compensation is directly linked to the actual energy cost savings.[11]

---

11. https://www.energy.gov/femp/energy-service-companies#qualified

CHAPTER 5

EQUIPMENT SELECTION

> "Everything is based on a simple rule:
> quality is the best business plan, period."
>
> — John Lasseter

According to the Electric Power Research Institute (EPRI), there are over 60 manufacturers of EV chargers, a.k.a EV Supply Equipment (EVSE), and some 300 makes and models of Level 2 and DC fast chargers on the EPRI Vetted Product List.[1] And when you consider that Tesla dominates with over 60% of installed charging ports,[2] it isn't difficult to conclude that there are too many suppliers chasing too few customers, and that the EVSE industry is ripe for consolidation. In fact, the dominoes are already starting to fall. As I write this in May 2024, fast-charging equipment pioneer Tritium DCFC

---

1. https://www.epri.com/vpl
2. https://evadoption.com/ev-charging-stations-statistics/us-charging-network-rankings/

has become insolvent after growing at a breakneck speed with more than 13,000 DC fast chargers sold into more than 40 countries, and buffered charging pioneer Freewire Technologies has also closed its doors. Product reliability issues coupled with increased competition and inability to turn profits eventually brought about the demise of these suppliers.[3]

So how do you sift through the noise to find those manufacturers who will provide excellent reliability and will support your equipment for the long haul? An obvious first step is to review the financial health of those who are publicly traded. Of these, *companies that have thriving business units in addition to EVSE are likely going to be more stable in the long run than those who rely completely on EV adoption and market growth to survive*. Also, given that many of the suppliers are based outside of North America, geopolitical risk and federal incentive requirements for domestic manufacturing should also be considered.

Once you have narrowed down companies that have staying power amidst inevitable industry consolidation, the next sift should be to look at how the chargers stack up when it comes to basic *legal and technical requirements* alongside *future-proofing* for the next generation of EVs to soon enter the market. And be sure to also review the capabilities of the chargers to overcome common failure modes exhibited by broken chargers, as discussed in chapter 9.

---

3. https://www.aumanufacturing.com.au/tritium-s-rapid-rise-and-collapse-is-over-goes-in-to-administration

LEGAL REQUIREMENTS

ELECTRICAL SAFETY

All EVSE must be tested by a Nationally Recognized Test Lab (NRTL) to Underwriters Laboratories (UL) standards 2594 (Level 2 AC chargers) or 2202 (DC fast chargers). You will likely need a copy of the manufacturer's UL listing certificates to include with your site plans when pulling permits.

WEIGHTS AND MEASURES

As with dispensing gasoline or other fuels, electricity must be accurately metered as it flows from the EVSE to the vehicle. As we learned from the previous chapter, units of energy are expressed in kilowatt-hours (kWh) and the price is stated as dollars per kWh ($/kWh). Each state has its own regulations pertaining to how this is to be done; however, all of them are based on Handbook 44, published by the National Institute of Standards and Technologies (NIST).[4] In recent years, NIST Handbook 44 has included Section 3.40, "Electric Vehicle Fueling Systems," which specifies, among other things, price selection and display, what must be on the receipt, meter antitampering provisions, and accuracy testing. As I write this, few states other than California are yet able to physically test and certify equipment, and only 26 manufacturers have completed California's "CTEP" testing program so far.[5] You should thus limit your equipment search to CTEP-certified providers for any

---

4. https://www.nist.gov/publications/specifications-tolerances-and-other-technical-requirements-weighing-and-measuring-15
5. https://www.cdfa.ca.gov/dms/programs/ctep/ctep.html

site you are planning to install in California. As for the other states, most are yet working on their regulations, and those who have implemented regulations are grandfathering in existing charging stations for compliance well into the future.[6]

ADA (AMERICANS WITH DISABILITIES ACT)

EVSE should comply with the "Design Recommendations for Accessible Electric Vehicle Charging Stations" published by the U.S. Access Board.[7] Be sure that the EVSE you choose meets these recommendations as to the connector, card readers, electronic user interfaces, and switches and buttons, including the emergency start/stop button. Note also that the California Division of the State Architect has prescriptive regulations on ADA compliance for electric vehicle charging stations for sites in California.[8]

FIRE CODE

If the EVSE includes integrated battery storage (which is discussed in some detail later in this chapter), you will want to see if your state and/or city building code requires that the equipment be tested to UL standard 9540A. This is rare, and even when it is required the code sometimes includes exceptions for EVSE up to a

---

6. https://library.e.abb.com/public/4f3fa54d79c34b21b52d46180 19059ee/ABB_E-mobility_NTEP_CTEP_Metering_WhitePaper.pdf
7. https://www.access-board.gov/tad/ev/
8. https://www.dgs.ca.gov/DSA/Resources/Page-Content/Resources-List-Folder/Access-Compliance-Reference-Materials

specified kWh capacity of battery storage.[9] I bring this up because the National Fire Protection Agency handbook 855 makes numerous references to UL 9540A without explicitly requiring it for EV charging sites . . . at least, not yet.

"MUST-HAVE" FEATURES

Along with the legal requirements stated above, DC fast-charging equipment must have the following capabilities if you want to have a successful operation. The numbers in brackets refer to the EPRI Vetted Product List criteria, which I again highly recommend you download for reference.[10]

WIRED OR WIFI INTERNET CONNECTIVITY

Reliance on wireless data to connect chargers with payment gateways and network service providers is a preventable cause of charger failures. With apologies to cellular data providers, they simply can't be counted on for such critical communication links. I've seen far too many "broken" chargers fail in the field not necessarily due to hardware malfunctions but rather due to wireless network–related issues. Wherever possible, install chargers and card readers via direct wired (or secure WiFi) connections to the internet, and through routers and firewalls that you control.

---

9. https://up.codes/viewer/new_york/ny-fire-code-2020/chapter/12/energy-systems#1206.2
10. https://www.epri.com/vpl

EXTENDED ON-SITE WARRANTY AND SERVICES

Charging cables and connectors get dropped or run over, screens get vandalized, mice chew through underground cables . . . stuff just happens. Most hardware warranty programs provide two years of "parts-only" coverage. So find out what it will cost for not only parts but also on-site break/fix services, and what the service level agreement (SLA) provides in the way of turnaround time. Up-front investments made in extended warranties and on-site support is usually money well spent, especially if you are under obligation for high availability, such as the 97% uptime requirement of the federal NEVI funding program described in chapter 7. Check to see that your supplier has a good track record of uptime, and always call references before making your selection.

CABLE MANAGEMENT

When was the last time you filled your gas tank by backing in to a parallel parking stall? I suspect you never have. The liquid fuels industry realized over one hundred years ago that accommodating all auto makes and models requires a pull-through configuration. But somehow the EV industry has decided that everyone should instead back-in or nose-in to the charger. I suppose this made sense for the pioneering sites such as those which Tesla installed early on, where EV charging ports are always in the left-rear area of these vehicles. And it is understandable that parallel parking is a way to reduce the overall footprint and real estate costs of a charging facility. But with so many automakers now offering EVs, charging port placement has become the definition of chaos. Depending on the make and model, you will find ports located in the front or rear, driver or passenger sides, and even near the wheel well or in the nose of the vehicle.

To ensure charging access for everyone—including the emerging medium- and heavy-duty EV market segment—it is wise to find equipment that features either long charging cables with tethered steel cord retractors or cables hanging from sufficient height to reach anywhere on the vehicle.

AC CONNECTOR AND CHARGING INTERFACE
[EPRI LIST 1-2]

Although this book is primarily focused on DC fast charging, be aware that all non-Tesla Level 2 AC slow chargers provide the standard SAE J1772 connector interface. This is the way to go for the near-term if you are including Level 2 charging at your facility, because Tesla vehicles come equipped with an adapter to connect with SAE J1772 charging stations.

DC CONNECTOR AND CHARGING INTERFACE
[EPRI LIST 1-2]

There are three competing DC connectors. We begin with Tesla's NACS interface because it is rapidly becoming the de facto standard:

- **Tesla's North America Charging Standard** (a.k.a. "NACS" and "SAE J3400") is by far the most prevalent, with about 66% market share.[11] Until recently, all NACS charging facilities have been provided by Tesla for exclusive use by their customers at company-owned

---

11. See US Department of Energy AFDC database.

"Supercharger" sites. However, in late 2023 Tesla opened up the NACS technology for anyone to commercialize, and the auto industry has now rallied around what has become open standard SAE J3400 for future EV offerings. Tesla is also beginning to offer charging services to non-Tesla vehicles, with both NACS and CCS connectors provided at some charging facilities. The company has also inked contracts to sell their Supercharger EVSE equipment for large organizations to own and operate, again with the NACS connector as standard.[12]

- **CCS** (a.k.a. "SAE J1772" or "Combined Charging System") has for nearly a decade been the connector placed on all non-Tesla vehicles other than the Nissan Leaf and Mitsubishi Outlander. There are over a million cars on the road that rely on CCS to connect to fast chargers.[13] No matter the NACS momentum, CCS is a market not to be missed.

- **CHAdeMO** is the prevailing standard in Japan, and it is the DC fast-charging connector provided in all model years of the Nissan Leaf and Mitsubishi Outlander sold in North America. CHAdeMO is also the connector for some of the older Kia EVs too. The industry consensus seems to be that CHAdeMO is dying a slow

---

12. https://www.bp.com/en_us/united-states/home/news/press-releases/bp-boosts-ev-charging-network-with-100-million-dollar-order-of-tesla-ultra-fast-chargers.html. See also https://electrek.co/2023/11/13/tesla-signs-deal-gas-station-operator-sell-supercharger-directly/

13. See Experian's Automotive Consumer Trend Report: Q3 2023.

death in North America (noting that even Nissan's newer model EVs use CCS), and rare is the financial incentive program that requires installing chargers to this standard anymore.

I would recommend that you look for DC fast chargers that provide cables and connectors for both NACS *and* CCS at each parking stall. The second cable adds somewhat to the cost of the charger, but it is money well spent because the customer can simply choose the cable that suits the vehicle every time.

TESTING WITH MULTIPLE AUTOMAKERS
[EPRI LIST 1-2]

In theory, assuming both the vehicle and charger meet the SAE J1772 standard, then the two should be able to communicate over a charging cable to initiate the charge, allow the vehicle to dynamically control the speed of charging, and end the session. But this doesn't always work out according to plan out in the wild. For example, one of my clients agonized over many days to figure out why one specific vehicle make and model would always initiate and start a charge, only to abruptly terminate the session after a few minutes. After some analysis, it was determined that the faults occurred during the switchover from one onboard battery bank to the other. This was solved after some technical discussions between the automaker and charger manufacturer.

The point here is that there are as many charger manufacturers as there are EV varieties. So make sure your supplier can attest that equipment has been tested with a minimum of 10 different makes (automotive brands) of plug-in electric vehicles, as attested in the EPRI certification.

POWER QUALITY RESILIENCE [EPRI LIST 1-3]

As described in chapter 3, utilities don't always provide "clean" power. Supplied voltages can surge and sag during the course of the day as grid supply and demand fluctuates. You should find equipment that has undergone SAE J2894 testing to ensure uninterrupted operation when these random events inevitably occur.

OUTDOOR APPLICATION AND VANDALISM PROTECTION [EPRI LIST 2-1, 2-2]

Look for NEMA 3R or better outdoor ratings, and IK9 or higher vandalism protection testing. Ensure your service level agreement with the supplier includes rapid replacement of broken parts and that adequate inventory is on hand to supply them. Also, operating temperatures are tested under the required UL listings only to 104°F (40°C), so you should check with the supplier to ensure the extremes you're anticipating have been tested. And where necessary, see that the warranty covers any unusual altitudes at which the chargers may be operating, as many warranties are limited to 7000 feet (2000 meters).

NETWORK PROTOCOLS [EPRI LIST 3, 4]

I provide a deeper dive into network protocols in chapter 6; suffice it to say here that you should ensure the equipment and network can support OCPP 2.0.1 and OCPI 2.2 or higher. Most providers simply self-attest as to these qualifications; however, certification by the Open Charge Alliance is ideal. And, as with any electronic device, the ability to provide remote monitoring and to update firmware over the cloud are crucial for physical and cyber security.

PLUG AND CHARGE [EPRI LIST FE-9A]

The industry is consolidating around the international standard ISO 15118 to provide automated billing by simply plugging in the EV—without the need for paying with apps or credit cards. Tesla owners have enjoyed having this convenience for over a decade in the closed Supercharger network. The process requires use of encrypted security tokens to be passed between the vehicle, charger, and charging networks. Thus, as you can imagine, it gets significantly complicated when you have to securely manage transactions over dozens of automakers and perhaps hundreds of charging networks. Future-proof your facility by ensuring your equipment conforms to ISO 15118-3, and that the hardware is capable of implementing both 15118-2 and 15118-20.

FEE DISCLOSURE [EPRI LIST CA-1 TO 11]

I brought up the emerging Weights and Measures (NIST 44) legal requirements earlier in this chapter, and it is important to note that if you will be operating in California there are additional fee disclosure requirements there. I won't get into all of the details; suffice it to say California requires that you provide a physical display on-site to provide pricing per kWh, along with real-time cost updates on the screen. A credit card reader must also be provided, with the ability to print a receipt or send one electronically.[14] Note also that credit card

---

14. CCR Title 13, Chapter 8.3, paragraph 2360.

reader failures are a common cause of charger downtime, which I describe in chapter 9 along with steps you can take to reduce this risk.

"NICE-TO-HAVE" FEATURES

DYNAMIC LOAD BALANCING

Some of the more sophisticated chargers are able to optimize grid supply by dynamically allocating power among vehicles that are simultaneously charging. For example, a 300 kW charger with two cables and connectors might have a Chevy Bolt requesting 50 kW of power (the maximum rate at which this particular vehicle is able to charge) while a Kia EV6 is simultaneously requesting 230 kW. A charger without dynamic load balancing would split the available 300 kW into 150 kW per connector, leaving the Kia charging at the reduced 150 kW speed. In contrast, dynamic load balancing will get the Kia back on the road in less time by allocating all of the remaining 250 kW not being requested by the Chevy.

ENERGY STAR COMPLIANCE [1-5]

Many grant and rebate programs require Energy Star testing and certification for equipment reimbursements.[15] Most notable among them is the California Electric Vehicle Incentive Program, which phased in the requirement of Energy Star certification in 2024.[16] (Note that the federal NEVI program requires Energy Star

---

15. https://www.energystar.gov/products/ev_chargers
16. https://calevip.org/

certification for AC Level 2 equipment, but not for DC charging equipment.)

BUY AMERICAN PROVISIONS [FE]

If you will be seeking NEVI funding, the equipment must meet Buy American provisions for domestic manufacturing and components—or otherwise meet the requirements of the FHWA waiver expiring on June 30, 2024.[17]

MULTILANGUAGE DISPLAY [FE-5D]

The NEVI program, among other incentive programs, requires access for users that have limited English proficiency.

BATTERY BUFFERING

As you will recall, the Charging Profitability Matrix presented in the introduction of this book indicates that if the utility demand fee is greater than $10 per kW, then it makes sense to consider adding on-site battery storage to buffer the energy. Chapters 1 and 4 also described how your return on investment is directly correlated to the utility demand fee schedule. With battery buffering, you will pay more up-front for the on-site batteries—typically double the cost of a direct-grid charger—but this almost always accelerates time-to-market, and over time the savings can be incredible.

---

17. https://www.federalregister.gov/documents/2023/02/21/2023-03498/waiver-of-buy-america-requirements-for-electric-vehicle-chargers

Below are a few anonymized real-world examples of how property owners have turned to battery-buffered chargers to save on demand fees at NEVI-awarded sites.

	Utility	Demand Fee (kW)	Direct Grid (600 kW)	Buffered (200 kW)	Five Year Savings
Site 1	Utility 1	$10.50	$378.000	$126,000	$252,000
Site 2	Utility 2	$29.00	$870,000	$290,000	$580,000
Site 3	Utility 3	$16.50	$594,000	$198,000	$396,000
					$1,228,000

In all three examples, each location required about $200,000 more for the buffered chargers than if direct-grid equipment were to have been installed. However, in all cases this investment is easily recovered over the five-year investment horizon. But perhaps more impressive than the cost savings is how buffered charging enabled the projects to quickly get underway in the first place. Two of the sites were facing extended time delays and expensive impact fees to provision 600 kW service, whereas 200 kW in spare capacity was already available.

Put another way, and getting back to our water pressure analogy in chapter 4, charging from battery buffers is similar to how a water tower operates: a low-power pump is all that is needed to trickle water up the tower so it is ready to deliver high-pressure flow when demand is greatest. Taking the analogy further, having your own water tower on-site allows you use the water spigot already in place yet still provide a fire hydrant–like gusher when needed.

In general, you should look for the following in a battery-buffered charger:

- *Ratio of grid input vs. charger output.* The buffer can rapidly deplete if grid input is too low in relation to charging speeds delivered. I would recommend no more than a 1:4 ratio of grid input to aggregate charger output—for example, 75 kW minimum grid input to supply 300 kW combined DC charging speeds. Freewire Technologies's recent demise was due in part to their charger's unsustainable 1:7 grid-to-output ratio—the chargers would fail after a few back-to-back sessions because buffer replenishment couldn't keep up with charging demand. Expanding the buffer size can offset this risk in modest utilization scenarios, albeit with more cycles on the battery warranty, as described next.

- *Battery warranty.* Look for a battery buffer warranty that guarantees at least 70% state of charge retention over ten years. If there is a maximum throughput limit on the warranty (expressed in megawatt-hours or in battery cycles), you will need to do some modeling to estimate how many charging sessions and calendar years this will likely represent. Returning to the above bullet point, higher grid-to-charging ratios may save you on utility demand fees, but this will also cause deeper cycling of the battery and accelerated expiration of the battery cycle warranty.

- *Simultaneous charging and buffer replenishment.* Some of the more sophisticated buffered chargers can replenish on-site battery storage during those times when EV charging demand drops below grid input—such as at the tail end of a charging cycle.

- *Grid integration.* Some battery-buffered charging systems allow you to favor buffer replenishment during off-peak hours when energy costs are low, as described in chapter 4. Some are also able to sell stored energy back to the grid, or provide power to a building to reduce energy costs during peak hours or for emergency power backup purposes.

- *DC coupling.* Given that the grid is supplying alternating current (AC) power while the vehicle must charge and store direct current (DC), all fast chargers exhibit some energy loss—typically around 7% or so during this energy conversion from AC to DC power. So when it comes to battery-buffered chargers, look for those that boost the DC storage out to the vehicle directly as DC, rather than requiring additional conversions to AC and then back again to DC. Also, if you plan to integrate solar generation on-site, look for the ability to couple the solar DC output directly to the charger's battery buffer, rather than converting to AC and then back to DC.

EQUIPMENT REVIEWS

For those who want to see demonstrations of various makes and models of DC fast chargers, I would recommend the reviews posted by YouTuber "Out of Spec Reviews."[18] Online publisher Electrek occasionally

---

18. https://www.youtube.com/@OutofSpecReviews

publishes articles and reviews of chargers, too.[19] It is also useful to read the comments from EV drivers on the various equipment in the field, as reported at PlugShare and Google Maps.

FUTURE-PROOFING

Finally, let's consider how to optimize charging equipment selection so as to future-proof the site.

AT LEAST 150 kW SUSTAINED CHARGING SPEEDS

Automakers are increasingly building faster charging capabilities into their EV offerings. So there is really no sense in offering DC fast charging at any speed lower than 150 kW per connector, as that is the speed at which the vast majority of new EVs can accept—with many able to charge as high as 300 kW for at least a portion of the charging session. Sustained charging speeds in excess of 250 kW is known as *ultrafast*, and it is accomplished on the vehicle side by turning to higher voltage architectures for the powertrain and battery storage.

By way of background, first-generation EV batteries, such as were produced for the Nissan Leaf and Chevy Bolt a decade ago, could only charge at speeds approaching 40 kW. This was due to a 400 volt DC architecture on the car. Over the next half decade, 400 volt DC was optimized to yield charging speeds of up to 150 kW, which is, not coincidentally, why the NEVI and other financial incentive programs require at least this speed of EV chargers to be installed. The vast majority of EVs on the road today are based on 400 volt DC systems and are

---

19. https://electrek.co/

thus limited in charging speed to approximately 150 kW on average.[20]

In 2019 the fast-charging game changed when Porsche premiered its Taycan sports car, which features an 800 volt DC architecture and sustained charging speeds up to 270 kW. Under optimal conditions, the Taycan can connect to a 300 kW charger and bring the state of charge from five to 80 percent in just 23 minutes.[21] Since then, other automakers have begun to produce vehicles with 800 and 900 volt architectures too, most notably Lucid, Tesla, Kia, and Hyundai. Owners of these EVs can also charge at lower speeds on legacy 400 volt equipment; however, given a choice they will charge at ultrafast chargers providing at least 250 kW output power.

The quandary you face in future-proofing a new facility with 250 kW or higher speed chargers is that not only are they more expensive than 150 kW chargers but the resulting utility demand fees will also increase, potentially rendering a return on investment impossible to achieve. Again, use of battery-buffered chargers and direct DC-coupled solar microgrids are an emerging way to mitigate these costs, albeit with higher up-front capital requirements.

OVERSIZE UTILITY MAKE-READY

Where possible, see if your utility can oversize the transformer and switchgear in preparation for additional

---

20. Efforts are underway to develop a "MegaWatt Charging System" standard for the truck and bus industry. For more details, see https://www.charin.global/technology/mcs/
21. https://newsroom.porsche.com/en_US/products/world-premiere-porsche-taycan-sports-car-sustainable-19176.html#

chargers and faster charging speeds. Most utilities are reluctant to do this, however, because of the higher costs associated with large transformers. You may find an increased make-ready or impact fee associated with this request, but it is worth it if you anticipate a ramp-up of charging activity over time. Another option, in some circumstances, is to provide your own transformer under "Primary Service" rate tariffs.

STUB UP ADDITIONAL CONDUITS

Prepare for additional growth of the charging facility by including underground conduits for additional charger stalls and by pouring ancillary equipment pads. Doing this also demonstrates to the utility that you are serious about needing more power as EV adoption increases, and thus they might be more agreeable to oversizing transformers from the start.

CHAPTER 6

CHARGING NETWORK SELECTION

"Look after the customer and the business
will take care of itself."

— Ray Kroc

Charger uptime and customer satisfaction are highly dependent on the quality of software and services provided by your charging network. There are many to choose from and are known as Charge Point Operators, or CPO for short.[1]

Core CPO roles and responsibilities include the following:

- Maintaining a customer helpline via phone and/or mobile app.
- Initiating and completing transactions.

---

1. Not to be confused with ChargePoint, Inc.—one of the earliest and larger CPO companies.

- Processing and remitting payments to the site host.
- Monitoring charger health and reporting faults to hardware suppliers.
- Reporting charger utilization statistics to site host and to utilities.

Additional services offered by CPO networks often include the following:

- Turnkey hardware + software supply and support.
- Roaming arrangements with other networks.
- Plug & Charge (ISO 15118) capabilities.
- Assistance in obtaining incentive funding.

OCPP: OPEN CHARGE POINT PROTOCOL

The common standard underpinning all CPO networks is the ability to connect and control any networkable charging hardware by way of the Open Charge Point Protocol, or OCPP. This open standard is published and maintained by the Open Charge Alliance, which has over 330 members spanning all sectors of the industry.[2] Of course, as with any open standard, interoperability is not always guaranteed. It is thus common practice for each CPO to maintain a list of chargers that have passed internal compatibility testing and for which the CPO is comfortable supporting in the field. On a broader scale, the Open Charge Alliance has recently begun offering

---

2. https://www.openchargealliance.org/about-us/about/

certification programs for hardware and network providers in an effort to ensure compatibility across all platforms.

You should thus only select a hardware + CPO software combination where both suppliers can produce an OCPP test report certifying compatibility with each other. If one or both can additionally produce Open Charge Alliance certifications then all the better, because this ensures you can more easily switch to another CPO in the future if you aren't happy with the level of service you are receiving.

CPO BUSINESS MODELS

As I write this, there are over 30 CPO networks in North America. And more keep showing up on my radar all the time. So how do you decide which one to trust with this vital service?

HYBRID HARDWARE + SOFTWARE OFFERINGS

Most CPO business models take a hybrid approach, offering "white label" branded software (both mobile app and web based) and call center support services to site hosts, while also owning and operating their own network of charging stations. Many of the networks listed on www.PlugShare.com fall into this category.

The upside to contracting with these providers to remotely manage your charging facility is that they are in the same boat with you: if the software has bugs or if the call center staff is incompetent then they also suffer from unhappy customers and lost profitability at sites that they own. As a result, these hybrid CPO companies tend to have advanced software and great relationships with the electric utilities, and they provide very reliable 24/7 support operations. On the other hand, the downside with hybrid CPOs is that they are inherently competitors with you. I have clients who have expressed concern that their CPO network will sometimes bid on the same competitive RFP solicitations that my client is also trying to win, with the added challenge that the CPO knows my client's charging volumes and revenues.

SOFTWARE-ONLY OFFERINGS

There are a handful of software-only networks. These take a little effort to identify (as they mostly operate behind the scenes for others), but they are worth investigating if you are making any sizable investment in a multiple-site charging strategy. With these solution providers, you are generally on your own for customer support operations, but they are nevertheless with you along the way, providing tools for your call center staff to remotely restart the equipment and perform other troubleshooting tasks. As with hybrid offerings, software-only providers also perform OCPP testing with many of the charger manufacturers and can escalate problems with broken equipment and warranty claims as they arise.

Some software-only networks also offer source code packages from which you can branch your own custom software, providing updates to the core from time to time. My experience has been that such core software packages can certainly check all of the required boxes to support your own charging network, but they may not have the depth of reporting or network-to-network roaming capabilities (known as OCPI or Open Charge Point Interface), which are available with full-service CPO solutions.

VETTING AND SELECTION

When it comes to selecting a CPO, bigger isn't necessarily better, and *regional players* can sometimes provide local knowledge and relationships that add value to your business. For example, there are 35 air quality districts in California, each with EV infrastructure rebate programs that come and go with the ebbs and flows of budgetary allocations. If this market is important to you, then a tie-up with one of the California-based CPOs might help you stay on top of these competitive grant programs. There are likewise some excellent CPOs based in Canada and the New England, Mid-Atlantic, and Central regions to consider.

That being said, if you want a fully turnkey hardware + software solution, then the big CPOs have the clout and balance sheets to stock and ship what you need, including getting spare parts out into the field quickly. They also have relationships with nationwide electrical contractors for on-site maintenance and troubleshooting.

No matter which route you choose, it is always a good idea to perform some due diligence on the CPO before signing up. Get a list of their charging facilities and then poke around on PlugShare and Google Maps to see what comments EV drivers have posted about site uptime and call support responsiveness. You might also want to have someone drive up with an EV to a few of the sites, call the support hotline listed on the charger, see how quickly the phone is answered, and get a sense if the representative is able to answer questions about how to connect the charger, take payments, etc.

LEGAL AND INCENTIVE CONSIDERATIONS

As I mentioned in the Weights and Measures subheading of chapter 5, many states are adopting NIST Handbook 44 requirements for accurately dispensing energy into electric vehicles. Among other things, your hardware + CPO combination must support the following:

- Pricing display in kWh to three decimals (four decimals in California).
- Dynamic time-of-use pricing (if desired).
- Fees for parking time or other additional costs (if desired).
- Display of cumulative cost of charging at minimum five second intervals.
- Printed or electronic receipts meeting NIST 44 specifications.
- Physical credit cards with chip, swipe, or tap.
- "Charging for All"—no membership or app required.

In many cases, the CPO must also be capable of assisting you with providing anonymized charging data to incentive funding sources at regular intervals *in the specified format required by each funding source.* This is no trivial task. There are a myriad of utility and government incentive programs out there, each requiring that the Excel or CSV file be formatted in a specific way, including data fields that require complex calculations on cumulative energy dispensed over specified periods of time. Utilities and government programs that require such reporting will typically have an approved list of CPOs who have demonstrated the ability to generate these reports. You can generally count on the large nationwide CPOs to be on all approved lists, with the smaller ones being able to get on them with some time and coordination, as needed.

Also, in an effort to avoid rolling "brownouts" during periods of high electricity demand, some utility incentive programs are now requiring that chargers be configured to throttle back or cease charging in response to Automated Demand Response (ADR) events. Before selecting a CPO, you should check to see if they can meet the requirements of OpenADR 2.0, and if the EVSE hardware you have chosen can accommodate commands by the CPO when such events take place.

CHAPTER 7

FEDERAL NEVI & CFI FUNDING

> "When a dollar stays in your community it is still a dollar. But when it goes first to Washington, it is diluted and trimmed and comes back a mighty small piece of change."
>
> — Dr. A. C. Sudan

This chapter describes a massive $7.5 billion five-year initiative that is currently underway to provide up to 80% of the cost for installing and operating DC fast-charging facilities. It is funded by the *federal* government in the form of *grants to each individual state* to design and carry out, and it is mostly targeted toward building charging stations located nearby highways or on properties owned by government entities.[1] This was authorized in late 2021 by the US Congress as part of the Bipartisan

---

1. There are (and likely will continue to be) some discretionary exceptions, such as a recent RFP to fix broken chargers out of this funding allocation.

Infrastructure Law. The two EV infrastructure programs consist of $5 billion allocated under the National Electric Vehicle Infrastructure (NEVI) Formula Program, and $2.5 billion allocated under the Discretionary Grant Program for Charging and Fueling Infrastructure (CFI).[2]

The NEVI program is being administered by the federal DOE-DOT Joint Office of Energy and Transportation, which has approved the plans submitted by all of the 50 states, along with DC and Puerto Rico.[3] The CFI program is being administered by the federal DOT alone.

Both NEVI and CFI grants provide up to 80% government cost-share of the costs to procure, install, and maintain EV charging facilities. These programs follow *EV Charging Minimum Standards*, which have become part of the Federal Highway Administration regulations,[4] specifying a number of requirements as to the following:

- **Location:** Must be along specified "Alternative Fuel Corridors," within 50 miles of each other, available 24/7 year-round, with uptime of 97% or greater.
- **Capabilities:** Must have at least four network-connected DC fast-charging ports, each able to continuously charge at speeds of at least 150 kW up to 920 volts using CCS-compliant connectors.[5]

---

2. https://www.transportation.gov/urban-e-mobility-toolkit/e-mobility-infrastructure-funding-and-financing/federal-funding-programs
3. https://driveelectric.gov/state-plans/
4. https://www.ecfr.gov/current/title-23/chapter-I/subchapter-G/part-680
5. Note that many states have begun to require open standard J3400 (Tesla's NACS) connectors in addition to the CCS requirement. See chapter 5 for background on this standard.

- **Payments:** Requires secure payment methods, without membership requirements, with access to users who are disabled (ADA) or have limited English proficiency.
- **Security:** Must be equipped with physical and cyber security strategies.
- **Installation:** Requires EVITP qualified electricians,[6] with federal prevailing wage consideration.
- **Interoperability:** Sites must support Plug & Charge (ISO 15118), OCPP, OCPI, and network switching.
- **Reporting:** Quarterly data submittals are required from each site host.

APPLYING FOR NEVI GRANTS

Joint Office funds are disbursed and administered at each state highway DOT office via a competitive bidding process. Below are some tips on what you should do to narrow down locations that might make sense for NEVI, and how to get into the competitive process for those sites that do.

ROI CONSIDERATIONS

Referring again to the Charging Profitability Matrix provided in the introduction of this book, there are areas in the country where either the anticipated traffic is so low[7]

---

6. https://evitp.org/
7. https://cowboystatedaily.com/2023/02/21/uh-oh-24-million-in-fed-money-to-build-wyoming-charging-stations-may-not-be-enough/

or utility rates are so high[8] that there is simply no return on investment to be made in EV charging alone—even with 80% of the costs being covered by taxpayer funds. If so, consider if there are other compelling reasons to host EV charging, such as increasing foot traffic to your business.

READ THE STATE PLAN AND PRIOR RFPs

The Joint Office website provides links to download each approved state plan by fiscal year.[9] These plans offer insight on specific locations to be targeted for funding, where existing charging infrastructure exists or is lacking, and objectives of the state for use of the NEVI funds. Pay close attention to how your proposed sites might align with state objectives in areas such as providing charging in underserved communities, in supporting tourism, etc.

State plans include maps of Alternative Fuel Corridors, including which highways are being targeted by fiscal year funding allocation. Your state may have already completed one or more rounds of funding, thus the geographical areas you are targeting might no longer be eligible.

GET INVOLVED

Almost all states have websites dedicated to their EV programs. These websites often include the ability to be added to *partnering directories* where you can get acquainted with those suppliers, contractors, community organizations, utilities, and local governments who

---

8. See chapter 8 for detail on utility rates and ROI.
9. https://driveelectric.gov/state-plans/

are also focusing on EV charging. Make calls and set up meetings to determine with whom you will partner for the next RFP. This is a must-do step because, apart from Tesla and a few of the larger charging networks, no one wins NEVI solicitations without partnering arrangements between the site host, hardware supplier, network software supplier, and a general contractor who has credibility with the state DOT. Letters of support for your intended project from utilities, municipalities, and subcontractors are also vital to include in your application.

LEARN HOW OTHERS PLAY THE GAME

Consultancy EV Adoption has been tracking state NEVI solicitations and awards, providing useful analysis and statistics on who is winning, and why. A subscription to the NEVI database and newsletter is money well spent, especially if you are considering sites in multiple states.[10]

GET APPROVED TO BID

A vetting process is required by some states before you can bid. This is because each state DOT is on the hook for at least five years to ensure all of the sites operate in accordance with federal requirements. If you fail, the state DOT also fails, which could be costly for the taxpayer to remedy. But again, that's where the partnering directory can be helpful in teaming up with primary contractors who have the credibility to submit winning bids, along with hardware and software providers with proven track records of charger uptime.

---

10. https://evadoption.com/subscription-nevi-basic-dates/

You will want to get on the state DOT email list to receive notifications of webinars and competitive RFP dates. Importantly, I have found that state DOT offices welcome the opportunity to visit with potential applicants in advance (and sometimes even during) the RFP process to answer questions and to clarify the key objectives the state has in mind for leveraging these federal funds.

TIPS ON RESPONDING TO THE RFP

Most of the NEVI RFPs that I've reviewed include scoring rubrics that weigh heavily on applicant cost-share and on site readiness. State highway officials are accustomed to leveraging federal funds for maximum impact across as wide a geography as possible, and to completing projects as soon as practical. Take a close look at the ROI modeling presented in chapter 8 and then develop your own model, including other non-NEVI incentives that could be layered onto the subject properties. You may find that seeking a smaller government cost-share will tip the scoring in your favor yet still provide a reasonable return on investment. Having site plans already drawn up, permits in hand, and written utility commitments will also score well in the readiness category.

APPLYING FOR CFI GRANTS

Unlike the $5 billion NEVI program, which is administered by the states and targeting the *private* sector, the $2.5 billion Charging and Fueling Infrastructure Discretionary Grant Program (CFI) is administered by the federal DOT alone via nationwide funding opportunities, and it mostly targets the *public* sector.[11]

Applications for the first round of funding closed in June 2023, and $622 million in awards to 47 applicants were announced in January 2024.[12] In 2023 the federal DOT also awarded $149 million toward replacing broken chargers, as I describe in more detail in chapter 9.

If your potential charging site is a likely candidate for CFI funding, I would encourage you to periodically visit the FHA's website, which is dedicated to this program,[13] and to join your local Clean Cities Coalition to get on their mailing list for notifications of funding opportunities such as these.[14]

---

11. https://www.fhwa.dot.gov/environment/cfi/
12. https://www.fhwa.dot.gov/environment/cfi/grant_recipients/
13. https://www.fhwa.dot.gov/environment/cfi/resources/
14. https://cleancities.energy.gov/

CHAPTER 8

MODELING RETURN ON INVESTMENT

"If you fail to plan, you plan to fail."

— Benjamin Franklin

As I write this, retail pricing at public DC fast chargers around the country is ranging between 33 to 69 cents per kWh, while the average cost of commercial power is hovering around 12 cents per kWh.[1] On the surface, this would appear to be similar to buying wholesale gasoline at $1.20 while offering it for $6.00 at the pump. With a markup of 3x to 5x on power, it would seem that those who offer public charging are making bank, right? Well, maybe not. As I shared in chapters 1 and 4, even the most attractive margins on energy dispensed can be overwhelmed by utility demand fees and up-front capital expenses, while on the other hand tax credits,

---

1. https://www.eia.gov/electricity/state/

grants, and incentives can significantly enhance overall project ROI, too.

MODELING TOOLS

As you work toward putting together your own ROI model, here are some resources for prepackaged spreadsheets to get you started.

NREL EVI-X MODELING SUITE

The National Renewable Energy Laboratory (NREL) offers many free tools, most of them geared toward assisting public policy and utility planners with EV adoption planning. The one of particular interest to prospective EV charging facility site hosts is the *Electric Vehicle Infrastructure Financial Analysis Scenario Tool* (EVI-FAST) Excel workbook.[2] This model leverages prior government financial modeling performed for the hydrogen vehicle refueling industry,[3] and it includes a myriad of inputs and variables to produce some useful graphs and tabular outputs.

The challenge with EVI-FAST is that it is a proverbial "black box" when it comes to getting your head wrapped around what is going on with the calculations and cell interactions. Use of the file requires accepting a somewhat onerous software use agreement, and I frankly haven't met anyone who relies on EVI-FAST for actual site ROI evaluation. That being said, the input and output prompts in EVI-FAST have been helpful for me and my clients as we determine elements required for custom

---

2. https://www.nrel.gov/transportation/evi-x.html
3. https://www.nrel.gov/hydrogen/h2fast.html

analysis of the sites we are evaluating. In any event, you have nothing to lose by giving EVI-FAST a try.

OBJECTIVE ENERGY ROI MODEL (FREE!)

My approach is to provide clients with a simplified and customizable Excel workbook, which is designed to be a straightforward first pass for sanity checking a potential charging site. It incorporates only the essential metrics found in the NREL model. I also include the ability to compare a number of scenarios side by side, such as optional utility rate schedules, and *direct-grid charging* versus increasingly popular *battery-buffered charging* options to mitigate utility demand fees while preserving retail margins (I discussed the difference between these two charging systems in chapter 5). There is much more that I plan to include in the model—such as annual site volume escalation, cost of capital, graphs, etc. But for now, you can essentially recreate my basic ROI model by following along with the hands-on deep dive later in this chapter.

Please drop me a note using the contact form at my website www.Objective.Energy if you would like a free copy of this ROI model or would like to share with me what you have come up with.

ELEMENTS OF THE MODEL

Before diving into spreadsheets, let's revisit the Charging Profitability Matrix provided in the introduction of this book:

Potential Charging Volume (Chapter 3)	**Utility Demand Fees** (Chapters 4 & 5)
MIN. CRITERIA: 8+ sessions / charger / day	MIN. CRITERIA: $10/kW or lower
IF NOT: Consider building a smaller facility	IF NOT: Consider on-site battery buffering
Grants, Incentives, Tax Credits (Chapter 2)	**Energy Cost & Availability** (Chapters 3 & 4)
MIN. CRITERIA: Location qualifies for IRS 30C credit	MIN. CRITERIA: Retail margins of at least $0.25/kWh
IF NOT: Seek other reimbursements	IF NOT: Consider adding solar + storage

Amplifying what has been discussed in the above-referenced chapters, here are some things to keep in mind when building an ROI model.

TIERED RATE SCHEDULES

Most utilities group commercial customers into categories (such as small, intermediate, and large) based on monthly power utilization. Categorization is based on monthly peak grid demand (kW) and/or total energy consumed (kWh). In planning your charging facility, you have got to know the applicable schedule, and what the consequences will be if site utilization causes you to spill over into the next highest tier—which is a nice problem to have as demand increases for your charging facility, right? Well, maybe not. I've found that some utility rate schedules having zero (or very low) demand fees for "small" general service will significantly ratchet up demand fee rates for "medium" and "high" service tiers. In some instances, moving up to higher tiers also activates time-of-use rates, with punishing costs for energy use during weekday peak hours.

ALTERNATE RATE SCHEDULES

Utilities are increasingly offering special rate schedules or "riders" for DC fast-charging facilities, featuring significantly lower demand fees (some as low as zero), but usually with the trade-off of squeezing retail margins by way of higher energy costs per kWh dispensed. I touched on this in chapter 4, and I also model one such example later on in this chapter. When offered this choice, you will need to perform some analysis to determine the charging traffic required by each rate option to break even, and then see if there is flexibility in switching to the other rate(s) as volume picks up over time.

RETAIL MARGINS

As provided in the Charging Profitability Matrix, if you see a clear path toward eight or more charging sessions per day per charger, and the utility demand fees are reasonable (in the single-digits), then you will generally need to see *at least $0.25/kWh in retail margins*. When faced with high demand fees, you will need even higher markups on the energy dispensed, or otherwise find attractive up-front incentives to enhance ROI. Again, the utility might offer a choice between a demand fee schedule with low kWh energy costs or a nondemand schedule having higher kWh energy costs. If so, you will want to model both, as we do in this chapter.

You should have a good sense of the retail pricing of comparable fast-charging facilities in your area, and if you will be counting on other sources of revenues such as one-time connection fees, idle fees, advertising revenues, and Clean Fuel Standard credits. And, having read chapter 4, you should now have an understanding of the utility costs associated with the potential charging site—noting that utility demand fees should be modeled on a the worst-case (or nearly worst-case) scenario by aggregating demand should all chargers be dispensing at the maximum kW speed simultaneously at some point during the billing cycle. Note also that most of my clients separate their energy costs per kWh (an element of gross margins) from the demand fees per kW (viewed as a monthly operating expense), but this is up to you.

INTANGIBLE BENEFITS

According to analysis by geospatial technology provider Korem, on average, EV drivers spend $1 per minute at local stores while recharging, while spending considerably more time in stores or restaurants than other customers.[4] And offering charging services is a good way for site hosts to build customer loyalty.

Thus, anticipated increase in your surrounding retail businesses might be an additional metric to include in the mix.

OPERATING EXPENSES

In addition to the monthly costs inherent with any property (such as site acquisition/leasing, taxes, maintenance, security, lighting, etc.), you may wish to also include these items into your model:

- Utility demand fees (if you don't account for these within retail margins).
- Charging network fees (see chapter 6).
- Fuel excise taxes, if not passed on to the consumer.

---

4. https://youtu.be/34Ad2YnBc-I. See statements at 1:10 and 1:47.

- On-site extended warranty and support agreements.
- Credit card processing fees.
- Charger efficiency losses (typically 7% for the AC to DC inversion).
- Charger parasitic loads (check the charger's EnergyStar report or spec sheet).
- Data connectivity.
- Nonenergy utility fees (meter & billing, etc.).

CAPITAL AND UP-FRONT EXPENSES

In addition to the cost of the chargers, shipping, engineering, permitting, and installation, remember to include these into your model:

- Utility make-ready costs: transformer upgrades, impact fees, etc.
- On-site commissioning by the charger OEM and network software providers.
- Offsetting grants, tax credits, and utility incentives (see chapter 2).

BUILDING AN ROI MODEL

Let's now build a basic Excel workbook together. The hypothetical situation is a site having four chargers, each capable of 150 kW simultaneous charging speeds. It is located within a qualified Section 30C tax credit census tract, and the utility serving the site is Rocky Mountain Power (RMP). Our objectives are to determine the level of charging traffic required to break even within five years and what the overall ROI might look like after seven years.[5]

---

5. We don't account for the area's 12.5% excise tax, as presumably this will be passed on to the customer.

> **MONTHLY BILL:**
> **Customer Service Charge:**
> $53.00 per Customer
>
> **Facilities Charge:**
> $3.99 per kW
>
> **Power Charge:**
> **Billing Months** - June through September inclusive
> $13.27 per kW
>
> **Billing Months** - October through May inclusive
> $11.74 per kW
>
> **Energy Charge:**
> **Billing Months** – June through September inclusive
> 3.8878¢ per kWh for all kWh
>
> **Billing Months** – October through May inclusive
> 3.4405¢ per kWh for all kWh

Rocky Mountain Power Schedule 6

As is becoming increasingly common with public utilities, RMP provides commercial customers the option of a demand schedule ("Schedule 6") and a non-demand schedule ("Schedule 6A").[6] Schedule 6, provided above, features a wonderfully low energy cost at under $0.04 per kWh, but the combined facilities and power demand fee is higher than most: $17.26 per peak kW in the summer months and $15.73 per peak kW during the rest of the year. When it comes to Schedule 6, we will use an annual blended demand cost of $16.24 per kW. This is well above the Charging Profitability Matrix threshold of $10 per kW demand fees, so we know right off that there will have to be some offsets in other Charging Profitability Matrix quadrants if the proposed site is to become viable.

---

6. https://www.rockymountainpower.net/about/rates-regulation/utah-rates-tariffs.html

Optional Schedule 6A provided below removes the high demand fees, but with this comes a trade-off of really high time-of-use energy rates.

> **MONTHLY BILL**: (continued)
>   **Energy Charge**:
>   June through September inclusive
>   per kWh first 50 kWh per kW   28.1562¢
>   per kWh all additional kWh   10.3099¢
>   per kWh for all Off-Peak kWh   (8.3358) ¢
>   October through May inclusive
>   per kWh first 50 kWh per kW   24.9170¢
>   per kWh all additional kWh   9.1238¢
>   per kWh for all Off-Peak kWh   (7.3768)¢

Rocky Mountain Power Schedule 6A

Now, the astute reader will notice that although there are no demand fees with Schedule 6A, there actually *is* a demand component embedded into the energy costs. Do you see it? (Hint: it is expressed as "per kW" where everything around it is expressed in kWh.)

This optional schedule removes demand fees of the standard schedule, but at the same time it makes up for the revenue shortfall by causing us to be subject to a top-tier energy price of $0.25 to $0.28 per kWh for much of the billing cycle. In our scenario, this means that meeting the "first 50 kWh per kW" would be triggered only after first completing 525 charging events in the billing cycle.[7] We can thus assume that until EV adoption picks up, very little energy will be dispensed at the lower $0.10 (summer) or $0.09 (winter) tiers. We should also bear in mind that some charging will occur during off-peak hours. So for our purposes we will conservatively model $0.21 for the annual blended energy cost as we move into the retail margins calculation phase of the analysis.

---

7. Calculated as likely peak demand of 420 kW x "first 50 kWh" = 21 MWh, or 525 sessions of 40 kWh each.

In summary, the the good news is that optional Schedule 6A takes utility demand fees down to zero, while the bad news is that it places us on the edge of viability for the energy cost quadrant of needing $0.25 per kWh margins. Getting there will require retail pricing of at least $0.46 per kWh—which is on the high side of retail pricing in the area.

RETAIL MARGINS

Now that we have determined the trade-off between demand fees and energy costs, we should find out which schedule is optimal, and if other quadrants in the Charging Profitability Matrix can make up for the margin squeeze of Schedule 6A. We first compare revenues versus the cost of energy. (Note that cells highlighted in yellow are model inputs, and the model uses a 360-day year to provide for some maintenance downtime.)

Retail Margins

	Scenario A	Scenario B
	RMP Sched. 6	RMP Sched. 6A
Inputs from Main Tab:		
Average charges / day	32	32
Avg. dispensed (kWh)	40	40
Total sessions per year	11,520	11,520
Total kHw per year	460,800	460,800
Per-Session Revenues		
Dispenser Price (kWh)	$ 0.49	$ 0.49
Per-session fee	$ 0.99	$ 0.99
Per-session advertising	$ -	$ -
Idle / parking fees	$ -	$ -
Per- Session Costs		
Energy (kWh)	$ 0.036	$ 0.210
Network Fees (kWh)	$ 0.03	$ 0.03
Transaction fees (%)	4%	4%
Sales & excise taxes (%)	12.5%	12.5%
Annual Charging Revenues	$ 237,197	$ 237,197
Annual Charging Costs	$ 69,550	$ 149,729

As we see, the additional $0.17 per kWh of Schedule 6A versus Schedule 6 creates a significant headwind of approximately $80k on annual profitability. This also validates the Profitability Matrix, where retail charger pricing should provide at least $0.25/kWh in margins. So we now turn our sights toward comparing potential demand fee savings.

DEMAND FEE + OpEx

Next we look at utility demand fees alongside other monthly costs. I've cut ourselves some slack on peak demand observed by the meter during a billing cycle. This is because, given the charging curves of most EVs, the likelihood of four vehicles demanding the maximum 150 kW of power from each of the four chargers at the same time is remote. So I've modeled 420 kW as peak.

Monthly Operating Expenses

	Scenario A RMP Sched. 6	Scenario B RMP Sched. 6A
Utility Demand Fee		
Number of dispensers	4	4
Maximum charging speed (kW)	150	150
Potential simultaneous draw (kW)	600	600
Likely peak simultaneous draw (kW)	420	420
Utility demand fee ($/kW)	16.24	-
Demand fee:	$ 6,821	$ -
Other Monthly Costs		
Extended warranty, onsite support	850	850
Security, lighting, grounds	300	300
Data	150	150
Utility meter fee	170	170
Idle power draw	25	25
Total other costs:	$ 1,495	$ 1,495
Total Monthly Demand Fee + OpEx:	$ 8,316	$ 1,495
Total Annual Demand Fee + OpEx:	$ 99,790	$ 17,940

In comparing this annual demand fee estimate alongside annual charging costs provided earlier, there is approximately $80k saved on demand fees with Schedule 6A, while on the other hand there is approximately $80k of additional energy costs, too. So it's a wash, which isn't surprising, as RMP would have had to convince its regulators that the optional schedule would be revenue-neutral over the rate base. But as we shall see, EV fast-charging facilities break the mold, so to speak, especially when charger utilization is extremely high or low.

INCENTIVES

You may recall that I shared earlier in the book how *those utilities that provide the most generous up-front incentives are also among the ones with the highest rates for energy and power demand*. This is certainly true here, where $15.73 to $17.26 per kW demand fees are much higher than most.

Nevertheless, RMP does provide fairly generous incentive programs for EV charging facilities, including the following:[8]

- up to $42,000 toward the total costs of charger hardware, and
- up to $500,000 for utility make-ready costs.[9]

---

8. https://www.rockymountainpower.net/savings-energy-choices/electric-vehicles/utah-commercial-incentives.html
9. Site host must also cost-share, typically 25% to 50% of the costs.

Incentives

	Scenario A	Scenario B
Tax Incentives	*(Same in either scenario)*	
Fed. Section 30C	73,500	73,500
Fed. ITC (battery storage)	-	-
State & local credits	-	-
Total tax incentives:	73,500	73,500
Utility Incentives		
Make-ready reimbursement	117,750	117,750
Charger rebates	42,000	42,000
Total utiliy incentives:	159,750	159,750
Grants		
NEVI	-	-
Other grants	-	-
Total grants:	-	-
Total Incentives	233,250	233,250

CapEx

Our last analysis before putting it all together has to do with capital and up-front costs. Note these figures are roughly based on what I've seen around the country for direct-grid fast charger installations. They do not necessarily reflect the costs of the specific equipment you may wish to install, nor are they published numbers from RMP, or any other utility for that matter.

Capital Expenses		
Equipment	Scenario A	Scenario B
	(Same in either scenario)	
Chargers - 4x 150 kW	160,000	160,000
Materials	85,000	85,000
Total Equipment:	245,000	245,000
Site Preparation		
Engineering & Plans	8,000	8,000
Permitting	3,000	3,000
Transformer & line upgrade	72,000	72,000
Utility impact fees	61,000	61,000
Total Site Prep:	144,000	144,000
Installation		
Excavate, install, remediate	60,000	60,000
Commissioning	8,000	8,000
Total Installation:	68,000	68,000
Total Capital Expenses	457,000	457,000

MODEL OUTPUT

When the model is fully assembled, we see that using an *average of 8 charges per day per charger* does indeed make it a wash between the two rate schedules. Importantly, we see how incentive funds offset what would otherwise miss the mark in the Profitability Matrix when it comes to demand fees and energy costs.

DC Fast Charging ROI Model

<-- Model inputs in yellow cells

	Scenario A	Scenario B
	RMP Sched. 6	*RMP Sched. 6A*
Average charges / day	32	32
Avg. dispensed (kWh)	40	40
Annual		
Revenues	237,197	237,197
Charging Costs	(69,550)	(149,729)
Util. Demand Fees + OpEx:	(99,790)	(17,940)
Margin on Sales:	67,857	69,527
Capital Expenditures		
Total CapEx & Upfront Costs	457,000	457,000
Incentives	(233,250)	(233,250)
Net CapEx & Upfront Costs:	223,750	223,750
Cumulative Cashflow		
Year 1	(155,893)	(154,223)
Year 2	(88,036)	(84,695)
Year 3	(20,179)	(15,168)
Year 4	47,678	54,359
Year 5	115,535	123,887
Year 6	183,392	193,414
Year 7	251,248	262,941

For simplicity, what we have assembled here is a first-pass sanity check, without taking into account any number of things that belong in a complete ROI model, such as cost of capital, growth scenarios, etc.

Finally, let's determine what happens if we don't achieve the minimum target of 8 chargers on average per charger per day. Without the monthly demand fee overhead, optional Schedule 6A saves us from risks of low utilization—for example, if the site averages only 4 charging sessions per day per charger:

DC Fast Charging ROI Model
<-- Model inputs in yellow cells

	Scenario A	Scenario B
	RMP Sched. 6	*RMP Sched. 6A*
Average charges / day	16	16
Avg. dispensed (kWh)	40	40
Annual		
Revenues	118,598	118,598
Charging Costs	(34,775)	(74,865)
Util. Demand Fees + OpEx:	(99,790)	(17,940)
Margin on Sales:	(15,966)	25,794
Capital Expenditures		
Total CapEx & Upfront Costs	457,000	457,000
Incentives	(233,250)	(233,250)
Net CapEx & Upfront Costs:	223,750	223,750
Cumulative Cashflow		
Year 1	(239,716)	(197,956)
Year 2	(255,683)	(172,163)
Year 3	(271,649)	(146,369)
Year 4	(287,615)	(120,575)
Year 5	(303,582)	(94,782)
Year 6	(319,548)	(68,988)
Year 7	(335,514)	(43,194)

On the other hand, Schedule 6, with its lower cost of energy, is the way to go once volumes increase—for example, if the site averages as high as 12 charges per day per charger:[10]

DC Fast Charging ROI Model		
<-- Model inputs in yellow cells		
	Scenario A	**Scenario B**
	RMP Sched. 6	*RMP Sched. 6A*
Average charges / day	48	48
Avg. dispensed (kWh)	40	40
Annual		
Revenues	355,795	355,795
Charging Costs	(104,325)	(224,594)
Util. Demand Fees + OpEx:	(99,790)	(17,940)
Margin on Sales:	151,680	113,261
Capital Expenditures		
Total CapEx & Upfront Costs	457,000	457,000
Incentives	(233,250)	(233,250)
Net CapEx & Upfront Costs:	223,750	223,750
Cumulative Cashflow		
Year 1	(72,070)	(110,489)
Year 2	79,610	2,772
Year 3	231,291	116,033
Year 4	382,971	229,294
Year 5	534,651	342,555
Year 6	686,331	455,816
Year 7	838,011	569,077

---

10. Note that a more comprehensive model would take into account the lower-tier energy costs of Schedule 6A as "the first 50 kWh per kW" is satisfied each month in this high-utilization scenario.

CHAPTER 9

WHY SO MANY CHARGERS ARE BROKEN

> "Government does not solve problems;
> it subsidizes them."
>
> — Ronald Reagan

If you have done any research into EV charging, you have likely seen dire statistics when it comes to charger availability. If not, here are a few: According to a 2023 report from analytics company J. D. Power, over one-in-five EV drivers using public charging stations experienced charging failures or equipment malfunctions that left them unable to charge their vehicles.[1] And a recent *Wall Street Journal* report found that of the 126 non-Tesla stalls inspected in the Los Angeles region, 27% were out of order.[2] A study in California's Greater Bay Area produced a similar result.[3]

---

1. https://www.jdpower.com/business/resources/ev-leasing-volumes-poised-surge-tax-rule-makes-it-cheaper-lease-buy
2. https://www.wsj.com/tech/i-visited-over-120-ev-chargers-three-reasons-why-so-many-were-broken-7a5d3e45
3. https://papers.ssrn.com/sol3/papers.cfm?abstract_id=4077554

I'm going to briefly touch on the historical background as to how we arrived at this sorry state of affairs, and then share the practical measures that can be taken to make sure *your* site provides as close to 100% uptime as possible.

OVERSIGHT AND ACCOUNTABILITY

When you boil it all down, today's *non-Tesla* broken charger quagmire can be attributed to having too much money tossed around to *install* chargers without accompanying pressure to actually *keep them operational*. There were two principal actors on this stage:

FEDERAL AND STATE GOVERNMENTS

Funding for charging infrastructure got a huge boost in 2016 after Volkswagen settled with the Department of Justice and California over its "Dieselgate" emissions cheating scandal.[4] As part of the settlement, Volkswagen agreed to spend $10 billion fixing or buying back the faulty cars, $2.7 billion on addressing the air pollution it had caused; and $2 billion to build out a charging network and educate the public on EVs thorough its Electrify America (EA) subsidiary.[5] The upshot is that EA installed about 4,000 chargers all over the United states and Canada to pave the way in advance of the EV adoption we are now seeing take hold. Today, EA ranks as the largest fast-charging network after Tesla.[6] Some of

---

4. https://www.epa.gov/enforcement/volkswagen-clean-air-act-civil-settlement
5. https://www.electrifyamerica.com/our-plan/
6. https://evadoption.com/ev-charging-stations-statistics/us-charging-network-rankings/

the Volkswagen settlement funds were also distributed to the states for charging infrastructure development.

Unfortunately, although the settlement requires Volkswagen to maintain the stations, no enforcement mechanism has been put into place at either the federal or California levels, and to date no fines have ever been imposed.[7] As a result, the most recent J. D. Power report ranks EA as dead last in overall customer satisfaction.[8]

But things are starting to look up for EA. In its final cycle ZEV Investment Plan, which was submitted in October 2023, the company acknowledges that their charger reliability is poor, and that they will be focusing on retrofitting and refurbishing underperforming chargers.[9] Another good sign that EA network reliability should improve is that with a $450 million capital raise in June of 2022, it is no longer just Volkswagen but Siemens and possibly others who are steering the ship toward a profitable enterprise as a private company. And EA's new flagship "oasis" locations are getting rave reviews.[10]

Allow me to also say, in EA's defense, that for nearly a half-decade the EA network has essentially been thrust into the role of a nascent industry's interoperability crash-dummy as each automaker rolls out new EV platforms and architectures. As I stated before in our discussion on equipment selection in chapter 5, just because the vehicle and charger conform to the same industry

---

7. https://www.washingtonpost.com/climate-environment/2023/12/13/electrify-america-ev-charger-broken/#
8. https://www.jdpower.com/sites/default/files/file/2023-08/2023094 U.S. EVX Public Charging.pdf
9. https://media.electrifyamerica.com/assets/documents/original/1086-10202023PUBLICCycle4ZIPPlanCARBFINAL.pdf
10. https://arstechnica.com/cars/2024/02/heres-what-its-like-to-charge-an-ev-at-electrify-americas-new-station/

standards (esp. SAE J1772) doesn't mean they are always going to play well together. So the automakers have some culpability too by not adequately testing their EVs with a variety of chargers before releasing them out to the public. On top of this, many EA chargers are heavily used and simply got worn-out faster than anyone imagined.

WALL STREET

The other actor on the broken charger stage—who threw money around without requiring much in the way of accountability—is the public equity marketplace and top executives who were chosen to run companies in the emerging charging industry. The SPAC (Special Purpose Acquisition Company, a.k.a. "reverse-shell merger") craze of 2020 brought dozens of EV-related companies into the public equity markets. Most failed to live up to the hype, however.[11] There have been some notable bankruptcies in the vehicle space, but fortunately none of the non-Tesla charging networks have gone under. Some of the early networks were acquired (such as Volta, SemaConnect, GreenLots), while the others (notably ChargePoint, EVGo, and Blink) have seen market valuations plummet. EV charging equipment manufacturers have also taken a hit, with the exception of diversified manufacturers who have established profitable business segments outside of charging equipment alone.

This all plays into why so many chargers are broken. Flush with cash, senior management at these charging network operators went out on a buying spree to place as many stations on the map as they could, and as quickly

---

11. https://eepower.com/market-insights/electric-vehicle-spacs-trend-down-over-poor-performance-production-delays/#

as possible. As with Electrify America, the pressure was on to install the stations, with little consequence if the stations couldn't maintain uptime. According to the *LA Times*, while EV owners and automakers floundered, charger company executives were making bank. ChargePoint's board paid CEO Pasquale Romano more than $31 million over the last three years, plus stock options that vest valued at $44.8 million, while EVGo's chief executive Catherine Zoe was paid over $8 million.[12]

As with EA, however, things are turning around with the other large non-Tesla networks, too. I'm seeing a real effort to replace broken chargers, to improve network and vehicle telecommunications, and to quality-check equipment before deploying it in the first place.[13]

WHAT IS BEING DONE ABOUT IT

As part of the $2.5 billion CFI program, as further described in chapter 7, the US Department of Transportation recently awarded $149 million to repair and replace existing but nonoperational EV charging infrastructure. These funds are going to 20 states and will target 4,471 charging ports.[14] Each location will be upgraded to at least the NEVI requirements of four chargers capable of 150 kW power each, and each will be required to maintain year-round charger availability of at least 97%. While this initiative will certainly help,

---

12. https://www.latimes.com/environment/story/2024-01-24/california-ev-charging-stations-broken
13. https://www.youtube.com/watch?v=Fyik_5N8tFE
14. https://www.linkedin.com/posts/lorenmcdonald_this-morning-fhwa-released-the-award-recipients-activity-7153800422124605440-LtIR/

there are some fairness issues to be considered. As most of the broken chargers were installed with public funds in the first place, was it the right policy to go back to taxpayers to replace them when others who received subsidies have proven to be better stewards of public funds in keeping chargers maintained and operational (thus causing them to be shut out of this special 2023 CFI funding program)?

RELIABILITY TIPS FOR YOUR CHARGING FACILITY

Apart from downtime caused by vandalism, virtually all charger reliability issues in the field could have been avoided with better planning, engineering, and installation practices. When it comes to planning your new facility, the equipment selection advice provided in chapter 5 shouldn't be glossed over. Insist that your suppliers meet, at a minimum, the "must-have" requirements. Then, consider these *common failures* when in the site planning process:

POOR ENGINEERING AND INSTALLATION

Choose engineering firms that have prior experience with DC fast-charging facilities, and check references before hiring. Inquire if the electrical contractor assigned to the job is EVITP certified and that the electricians are also EVITP-trained.[15]

---

15. https://evitp.org/

DATA COMMUNICATION FAILURE

I touched on this in chapter 5, but one surprisingly common reason why chargers fail is because they can't always reliably connect to the internet. Charging equipment usually includes two or more SIM card slots for connecting the charger over cellular data to backend support and payment networks. This introduces an avoidable communication risk when compared to connecting the chargers over a *wired* connection to a firewall, router, and internet service. If a wired connection isn't possible, then your next best option is to provide secure WiFi service out to the chargers. Either way, providing your own internet service on-site will not only remove the common problem we see in the field with hiccups due to wireless data services, but it also will save you from burning a hole in your budget. This is because firmware programs on chargers are frequently being updated via huge data files, and many chargers now feature large screens for video advertising. All of this can add up to a small fortune if you are relying on wireless pay-as-you-go data plans.

CREDIT CARD READER FAILURE

EV chargers often feature credit card readers that are mounted near the display or are sometimes located at an external payment kiosk. But none of them are actually manufactured by the charger company themselves. The card reader is, essentially, a third-party device bolted onto the charger, provided with a source of power, and generally lives in a world unto itself. Unless the card reader is directly connected to the charger to authorize the charging session without reference to a network (this is rare), most readers are set up to connect to the internet by way of our nemesis described previously—that's right, a wireless data provider. So you should design the installation to run Ethernet cables for both the charger *and* the card reader separately, and properly firewall these connections out to the internet.

Unless the card reader is directly connected to the charger to authorize the charging session (again, this is rare), here is what actually happens behind the scenes when a customer uses a credit card to pay for charging:

1. The customer swipes, inserts, or taps a credit card/mobile device.
2. The card reader connects with a payment gateway for authorization.
3. The gateway sends approval to the charge point operator (CPO).
4. The CPO sends a signal to the charger to start.
5. When complete, the CPO turns off the charger, closes the session, and settles the financial transaction with the payment gateway.

As you can see, there are a number of steps where a hiccup in data communications will render the charger to be "broken."

MOBILE PAYMENTS FAILURE

As discussed in chapter 6, most charge point operators (CPO) provide mobile apps or dedicated secure websites for customers to initiate and pay for charging sessions, and many offer custom "white label" packages to customize an app and web payment portal with the site host's logo and design skins. These types of payments are more reliable than payments via a credit card reader because everything is handled between the CPO and payment gateway provider over the cloud—from secure data center to secure data center. The only time a cellular data network comes into play is when the customer selects the charger to initiate a session on his or her mobile device.

Nevertheless, when it comes to charger reliability, complete reliance on apps and payment portals alone isn't a great strategy either. Customers may have issues with mobile phone connectivity to begin with, and many are increasingly getting fed up with having to load so many CPO apps on their phones. This situation has gotten so bad that both California law and the federal NEVI funding program prohibit station operators from requiring apps or membership as a condition of offering charging services to the public. I suspect this will become commonplace with all legal and funding requirements nationwide.

One other source of mobile payment failure bears mentioning, and that is the potential for fraud. Scammers can potentially place a bogus QR code sticker over the genuine one to direct the customer to a nefarious website. The site then captures credit card and other sensitive information, leaving the customer not only open to fraud but literally out in the cold at the charging station, too. I haven't personally been made aware of such an occurrence in the EV charging space yet, but it is a risk to be addressed. To counter this, an emerging "sticker-over-sticker" risk mitigation strategy is to provide on-screen display of dynamic QR codes for each session; but not many CPOs and hardware providers are yet able to offer this.

IMPROPER MAINTENANCE

All DC chargers include cooling fans with air filters. Neglecting to maintain these airflow systems according to schedule is a fairly common cause of charger downtime. Some of the higher-speed DC chargers also include liquid cooling systems for cables and for internal battery buffers. These systems also require regular inspection and maintenance according to the manufacturer's schedule.

VEHICLE-TO-CHARGER COMMUNICATION FAILURE

As discussed in chapter 6, vehicle-to-charger communication should follow the industry standard SAE J1722, but there are nuances in how this standard has been applied by the various auto manufacturers and charging equipment suppliers. As mentioned in chapter 5, make sure that the charging hardware you have chosen has been tested with at least 10 auto manufacturers to reduce the risk of J1722 incompatibility issues in the field.

Physical cable damage can also become a source of vehicle communication failures. Look for chargers that feature cable management as described in chapter 5. It is also a good practice for your electrical contractor to be trained and qualified by the manufacturer to replace damaged cables and connectors, having at least one set on hand for each geographical region.

BROKEN SCREENS

Chargers become inoperative whenever a user interface screen is broken or otherwise unreadable. Vandalism and sun exposure are the two common causes of such failures. Ensure that the charger OEM is equipped to rapidly replace broken screens in the field.

GRID QUALITY SHUTDOWN FAILURE

DC fast chargers require a reliable source of grid supply and can sometimes trip internal breakers when input voltages dip or spike much beyond ±10% of nominal 480 V. This is understandable when you consider the cost of high-capacity power inverters and the sensitive electronics required to manage them. At the same time, many utility customers on 480 V three-phase service are powering motors, pumps, and other industrial equipment where temporary dips and spikes don't really matter. So utilities are not accustomed to 480 V customers complaining when there are momentary flaws in delivered voltage.

As discussed in chapter 3, where possible, you should locate sites near primary power distribution substations. This is your best way to mitigate risk of charging equipment shutdowns from grid quality issues. Even then, discuss with your utility provider the potential for dips and spikes, and what they are prepared to do if grid quality becomes a frequent cause of charger downtime. Investor-owned utilities are required to publish terms of service, which include metrics as to guaranteed voltage ranges. You should also find equipment that has undergone SAE J2894 testing to ensure uninterrupted operation when these random events inevitably occur.

CHAPTER 10

LEVEL 2 CHARGING CONSIDERATIONS

Much of the prior information covering DC fast charging is also relevant to AC Level 2 (L2) charging facilities, with some additional considerations.

ROI MODELING

As the costs to acquire and install Level 2 charging are but a fraction of those associated with DC fast charging, the Profitability Matrix discussed throughout the book is not necessarily applicable, and you will need to model your particular situation individually. In modeling your site, be especially aware of utility demand fees and time-of-use (TOU) energy rate schedules, as costs can quickly add up with multiple L2 chargers in operation at the same time!

UTILITY COST MITIGATION

When it comes to strategies for mitigating utility costs, special utility rate schedules for commercial DC fast-charging EV facilities, as described in chapter 4, are generally *not* applicable to AC charging. Thus, as with DC charging, you must consider other ways to cap the maximum demand placed on the utility grid by L2 charging if you want to reduce excessive demand fees.

As described in chapter 5, use of on-site battery buffering is one way to accomplish this; however, I have not found any integrated battery-buffered L2 charging systems in the market yet. But from a technical standpoint, interposing an off-the-shelf energy storage system (ESS) between the grid and L2 chargers is not a difficult thing to do. Many ESS offer the ability to prioritize accumulation of energy during utility off-peak hours and can cap monthly demand fees by regulating the maximum grid draw at any time during the billing period. You will encounter some energy losses (as high as 10%) from the ESS due to the the round-trip efficiencies required to store and discharge. Nevertheless, L2 sites in areas having high electric rate schedules will likely find that an investment in energy storage will pencil out when coupled with federal, state, and local incentives.

DYNAMIC LOAD AND BRANCH CIRCUIT BALANCING

The speed at which an EV can accept AC power varies by make and model, from as low as 2.9 kW to as high as 19.2 kW. To satisfy most EV owners, the charging power you should aim for is between 10 kW and 12 kW. This means that you should plan on providing 40 or 50 A service to each charger, which could be difficult to do if you need to install charging at multiple parking stalls and there isn't much spare capacity on the transformer. Methods to overcome this include the addition of on-site energy storage as described above, along with dynamic load balancing and the ability to throttle back charging speeds to cap the total grid (or branch circuit) demand.

NETWORKING

There is no need to pay up for networkable chargers and associated CPO networking service fees if you are going to offer charging for free. There are many low-cost, nonnetworkable chargers to choose from, in both wall mount and pedestal configurations, and some include the ability to restrict access to only those who have been given RFID cards or fobs. Removing the need for networking also reduces the likelihood of charger malfunction due to communication failures, as described in chapter 9. That being said, some utility incentive programs *require* networkable chargers and the submission of periodic charging activity reports. If so, see if the added costs for networking can be made up by such up-front reimbursement programs.

CHAPTER 11

THE ROAD AHEAD

> "History repeats itself.
> So you might wanna pay attention."
> — Quavo

My neighbor comes from a family who took part in early efforts to develop the Grand Canyon North Rim area as a tourist destination. The Utah Auto Club made the first organized expedition by car to visit this magnificent place in 1931, stopping in Kanab, Utah, for a final fill-up. There were eight cars carrying twenty-five people, and since there weren't enough cars along the route yet for anyone to invest in gas stations, my neighbor's great-grandfather stashed five-gallon cans of fuel along the dusty road leading to the North Rim to relieve range anxiety that these early motorists were facing.[1]

---

1. Oral interview with Dee Chamberlain, March 14, 2024; Unpublished memoirs of Mary E. Woolley Chamberlain, p. 149, in author's possession.

To put the above history into context, 38% of American cars were powered by electricity when my neighbor's great-grandfather was born.[2] So what we are witnessing today is simply a full-circle evolution of fuel and drivetrain technology, along with inevitable growing pains. I find it fascinating that many EV drivers today follow the same route of the intrepid 1931 Utah Auto Club by topping off in Kanab, Utah, (at a really slow 50 kW charger) before braving an approximate 150 mile roundtrip to the North Rim.

I hope you have enjoyed reading this primer on the promises and perils of offering electric vehicle charging. As stated before, my purpose with this book isn't to convince you to install charging. However, I will suggest, in parting, that now is probably good timing to get started, as the US market is approaching a tipping point where EV charging stations are getting busy enough to make money.[3] But even then, you must carefully select where to place the sites, and it is always best if the proposed charging facility is primarily designed to drive more customers to an existing retail business rather than the investment being reliant on deriving profits from the chargers alone.

Please feel free to contact me via my website www.Objective.Energy if you need clarification on the material presented, or if you need help with specific projects. I wish you well on your journey.

---

2. https://www.britannica.com/technology/automobile/Early-electric-automobiles
3. https://www.bloomberg.com/news/articles/2024-03-06/ev-charging-stations-in-the-us-are-finally-getting-busy

INDEX OF TERMS & ABBREVIATIONS

ADA   Americans with Disabilities Act

C-store   Convenience Store

CFI   Charging and Fueling Infrastructure Discretionary Grant Program
Federal funding program, described in chapter 7.

CPO   Charging Point Operator
Organizations providing hardware, software, payments, and customer support services. Some own and operate networks of charging facilities.

DCFC   DC Fast Charger

DOT   Department of Transportation

EA   Electrify America
Volkswagen subsidiary; second largest EV charging network in the country.

ESS   Energy Storage System

EVITP   Electric Vehicle Infrastructure Training Program
Industry consortium providing technician training courses and certifications.

EVSE   EV Supply Equipment
Generic term for chargers and ancillary equipment.

IOU   Investor-Owned Utility

INDEX OF TERMS & ABBREVIATIONS

L2   Level 2 Charging
AC charging equipment, typically 3 kW to 19.2 kW speeds.

LCFS   Low Carbon Fuel Standard
State regulations that require the lowering of carbon intensity in vehicle fuels.

kW   Kilowatt
A unit of electrical energy.

kWh   Kilowatt-Hour
A unit of power delivered or stored.

NACS   North American Charging Standard (Tesla)
Connector being adopted by all automakers in North America (a.k.a. J3400).

NEVI   National EV Infrastructure Program
Federal funding program, described in chapter 7.

NREL   The National Renewable Energy Laboratory
Provider of the EVI-FAST modeling software, described in chapter 8.

OCPI   Open Charge Point Interface
An open standard for network-to-network communications.

OCPP   Open Charge Point Protocol
An open standard for charger-to-network communications.

RFID   Radio Frequency Identification
A method of authorizing access by way of a physical card or fob device.

RFP   Request for Proposal
A competitive bid process, often utilized for grant funding programs.

RNG   Renewable Natural Gas
Natural gas from renewable sources; highly prized in LCFS incentive programs.

ROI   Return on Investment

SLA   Service Level Agreement
OEM warranty obligations as to turnaround time for maintenance and repairs.

TOU   Time-of-Use Utility Rates
Variable pricing schedules based on the day and time when power is delivered.

www.ingramcontent.com/pod-product-compliance
Lightning Source LLC
Chambersburg PA
CBHW070547090426
42735CB00013B/3093